The Silent Battle: My Story of Dealing with Chronic Anxiety

Gain Clarity, Build Resilience, Find Lasting Peace, and Achieve Work-Life Balance

Yuvraj Bhatnagar

The Silent Battle: My Story of Dealing with Chronic Anxiety
Gain Clarity, Build Resilience, Find Lasting Peace, and Achieve Work-Life Balance

© 2024 by Yuvraj Bhatnagar

This book is a memoir and a personal reflection. The author has shared his own experiences, insights, and observations to help readers understand and manage chronic anxiety. The information provided is not intended as medical advice or a substitute for professional consultation or therapy.

For permissions, collaborations, or inquiries, please contact:
Email: Yuvraj.bhatnagar@gmail.com

First Edition: 2025

Disclaimer

The contents of this book, *The Silent Battle: My Story of Dealing with Chronic Anxiety*, are based on the personal experiences, reflections, and insights of the author. This book is intended for informational and educational purposes only.

It is not a substitute for professional medical advice, diagnosis, or treatment. If you are experiencing symptoms of anxiety, depression, or any other mental health condition, please consult with a qualified healthcare provider or mental health professional.

The author and publisher have made every effort to ensure that the information presented in this book is accurate and reflective of personal experiences at the time of writing. However, individual experiences with anxiety and coping strategies may vary. Readers are encouraged to seek personalized support and professional guidance where necessary.

The author and publisher disclaim any liability or responsibility for any loss, damage, or disruption caused or alleged to be caused directly or indirectly by the information contained in this book.

Table of Contents

THE SILENT BATTLE: MY STORY OF DEALING WITH CHRONIC ANXIETY

GAIN CLARITY, BUILD RESILIENCE, FIND LASTING PEACE, AND ACHIEVE WORK-LIFE BALANCE

YUVRAJ BHATNAGAR

Made with ♥ on the Notion Press Platform
www.notionpress.com

Contents

Preface

The Silent Battle: My Story of Dealing with Chronic Anxiety
Gain Clarity, Build Resilience, Find Lasting Peace, and Achieve Work-Life Balance
Yuvraj Bhatnagar

The Silent Battle: My Story of Dealing with Chronic Anxiety

Gain Clarity, Build Resilience, Find Lasting Peace, and Achieve Work-Life Balance

This book is a memoir and a personal reflection. The author has shared his own experiences, insights, and observations to help readers understand and manage chronic anxiety. The information provided is not intended as medical advice or a substitute for professional consultation or therapy.

For permissions, collaborations, or inquiries, please contact:
Email: Yuvraj.bhatnagar@gmail.com

First Edition: 2025

Disclaimer

The contents of this book, *The Silent Battle: My Story of Dealing with Chronic Anxiety*, are based on the personal experiences, reflections, and insights of the author. This book is intended for informational and educational purposes only.

It is not a substitute for professional medical advice, diagnosis, or treatment. If you are experiencing symptoms of anxiety, depression, or any other mental health condition, please consult with a qualified healthcare provider or mental health professional.

The author and publisher have made every effort to ensure that the information presented in this book is accurate and reflective of personal experiences at the time of writing. However, individual experiences with anxiety and coping strategies may vary. Readers are encouraged to seek personalized support and professional guidance where necessary.

The author and publisher disclaim any liability or responsibility for any loss, damage, or disruption caused or alleged to be caused directly or indirectly by the information contained in this book.

Table of Contents

ABOUT THE BOOK

Imagine waking up every day with an invisible weight pressing down on your chest, your mind trapped in an endless loop of "what ifs" that drain your energy and joy.

That's what chronic anxiety feels like an unrelenting storm inside, even on the calmest days.

But what if this storm didn't have to define you or your loved ones?

What if anxiety could be understood, managed, and softened into a voice in the background that no longer dictates every thought and decision?

This book is a raw, honest exploration of anxiety; not a story of defeating an enemy, but of learning to live alongside it, to navigate its challenges, and to create a life of clarity, resilience, inner peace, and balance whether at work, at home, or in relationships.

An estimated 4% of the global population currently experience an anxiety disorder [1]

Whether you are struggling with anxiety yourself or watching someone you care about battle it, this book offers insights, tools, and hope for a more peaceful and fulfilling life.

Why This Book Stands Out

Anxiety doesn't just affect your mind. It seeps into every part of your life, especially your work. It clouds decision-making, drains confidence, and turns even routine tasks into overwhelming challenges. I know this firsthand.

For years, I juggled high-pressure corporate roles, struggling with self-doubt, overthinking, and the constant fear of failure.

I worked long hours, trying to prove my worth, yet anxiety made me question every achievement. Deadlines felt suffocating. Meetings triggered waves of self-doubt. The pressure to always perform left me exhausted. And no matter how much I succeeded on paper, I never felt "enough."

This book isn't just another guide on anxiety. It's a deeply personal journey woven with real-life struggles in the workplace, the relentless pursuit of success, and the toll anxiety takes on professional and personal life.

Through my lived experiences, I share actionable strategies that have helped me regain control, move past career anxiety, and finally find balance.

At its core, this book is about more than just managing anxiety. It's about gaining clarity in moments of doubt, building resilience to withstand life's pressures, finding inner peace amidst the chaos, and ultimately, achieving the work-life balance that once felt impossible.

If you or someone you care about are struggling with workplace stress, career anxiety, or the pressure to keep up in an always-on world, this book will serve as both a guide and a companion on the path to a healthier, more balanced life.

Although there are known, effective treatments for mental disorders, more than 75% of people in low- and middle-income countries receive no treatment. [2]

What sets this book apart is its unique blend of personal experience and practical strategies, guiding you to live peacefully with chronic stress without letting it disrupt your life or peace of mind.

Through my own journey, I share insights and tools that you can apply immediately. This isn't about temporary solutions or surface-level advice. It's about creating deep, lasting change for a calmer, more resilient life.

What You'll Gain

Anxiety can feel overwhelming, but it doesn't have to control your life. Whether you're struggling with your own anxiety or trying to support someone who is, this book offers real-life insights, practical strategies, and a path toward greater understanding and balance.

By reading this book, you will:

✓ Gain Clarity – Understand what anxiety really is, why it happens, and how it affects your thoughts, emotions, and daily life.

✓ Build Resilience – Learn how to manage anxiety during stressful situations, develop coping mechanisms, and strengthen your ability to handle challenges.

✓ Find Inner Peace – Discover ways to quiet the constant "what ifs," reduce overthinking, and create a sense of calm, even in difficult moments.

✓ Achieve Work-Life Balance – Learn to set boundaries, prioritize your well-being, and navigate work, relationships, and responsibilities without feeling overwhelmed.

This book isn't just about managing anxiety. It's about transforming your relationship with it, so you can live with greater confidence, fulfillment, and peace of mind.

A Journey of Transformation

This isn't just a book; it's a journey that invites you to reflect, engage, and transform. Each chapter ends with easy exercises designed to help you actively apply what you've learned. These are action steps to help you reshape your relationship with anxiety.

If you've ever felt trapped by anxiety, if you've ever wished for a way to break free, this book is for you. Together, we will explore the depths of anxiety and emerge stronger, wiser, and more in control of our lives.

If you or someone you care about has ever felt trapped by anxiety, if you've ever wished for a way to understand it better and offer real support, then this book is for you too. Together, we will explore the depths of anxiety what it feels like, how it shapes lives, and how to navigate it with strength and compassion.

Let's take that first step together. The journey to a life beyond the shadows of anxiety begins now.

?In 2019, 1 in every 8 people, or 970 million people around the world were living with a mental disorder, with anxiety and depressive disorders the most common [3].

? In 2019, 301 million people were living with an anxiety disorder including 58 million children and adolescents [3].

? The 2024 results of the American Psychiatric Association's annual mental health poll show that U.S. adults are feeling increasingly anxious. In 2024, 43% of adults say they feel more anxious than they did the previous year, up from 37% in 2023 and 32% in 2022. Adults are particularly anxious about current events (70%). [8]

? Around 828,000 employees suffer from work-related stress, depression, or anxiety annually. [10]

****

CHAPTER 1: INTRODUCTION

"Anxiety is like a rocking chair. It gives you something to do but gets you nowhere."

—Glenn Turner

For years, I lived in that endless rocking motion—pacing, overthinking, analyzing every scenario in painstaking detail, believing that if I just worried enough, I could control the outcome. Instead, I found myself paralyzed, exhausted, and drowning in a fear that had no off switch.

It was March 2002, just weeks before my final semester exams in my MBA program at JUMBA (Jiwaji University MBA). My classmates were busy preparing for campus placements, mapping out their careers with excitement. I, on the other hand, was barely holding it together.

By then, anxiety wasn't new to me. It had been creeping in for years tightening its grip with every self-doubt, every social interaction, every uncertain future.

Three months earlier, upon my professor's recommendation, I had started seeing a psychologist for my lack of confidence and the heart-pounding panic that seized me in the simplest situations.

The doctor reassured me I was improving, but I felt anything but better. As exam season approached, my anxiety surged into something darker and more consuming.

I tried reaching out, but no one truly understood.

"*It's just exam stress,*" my friends said.

"*You're just scared to leave home,*" my parents assumed.

"*It's career anxiety. Everyone goes through it,*" my psychology professor dismissed.

But deep down, I knew this was different. This wasn't just stress. It wasn't just nerves. It was something that took over my thoughts, my body, my sleep something that refused to let go.

As the days passed, my mind spiraled into an void of uncertainty. Every casual remark about the struggling job market sent me into a fresh wave of panic. Sleepless nights turned into weeks. My chest felt like it was locked in a vice. Every conversation, every decision felt like a test I was destined to fail.

Then came the darkest moments - the thoughts that whispered *"maybe it would be easier if I just didn't exist"*.

That terrified me.

I lay awake in bed, staring at the ceiling, my mind running circles around questions that had no answers.

One evening, desperate for relief, I sought out a family friend who referred me to a leading psychiatrist. By the time I reached Dr. Gupta's door, my hands were trembling. What if even he couldn't help me?

It was 9 PM when I arrived at his doorstep, barely holding back tears. I had no idea if he would understand or if he would dismiss me like everyone else. But as he listened. Really listened. I felt, for the first time in months, that maybe I wasn't imagining things. Maybe what I was going through was real. And maybe, just maybe, there was a way out.

And in that moment, his kindness felt like a lifeline. He prescribed medication to help me sleep and insisted I return with my parents immediately.

The next morning, as he explained to them what was happening, I realized how close I had come to breaking completely.

He called it a severe nervous breakdown one that, without intervention, could have ended disastrously.

That night changed many things.

I didn't find an instant cure. There was no magic switch that turned off my anxiety. But it was the beginning of something new - a journey of understanding what was happening to me, of learning how to manage chronic anxiety, of reclaiming the life I had almost lost.

This book is more than just a personal story. It's a window into the experience of living with anxiety, especially when it feels like no one truly understands. Anxiety isn't just occasional stress; it can affect every aspect of life—work, relationships, health, and even the motivation to keep going.

But there is hope. Anxiety doesn't have to define you. With the right tools and understanding, it is possible to regain control, find balance, and move forward.

If you or someone you care about has ever felt overwhelmed by worry, trapped in overthinking, or struggling in silence, then this book is for you.

You are not alone. And there is a path to clarity, resilience, and peace.

What Chronic Anxiety Feels Like

If you've ever found yourself endlessly replaying past conversations, worrying about things that haven't even happened, or feeling like a tightly wound spring with no clear reason, you're not alone. Chronic anxiety can feel like an invisible weight on your chest—a constant, draining companion whispering, "*What if?*" at every corner.

Unlike the usual pre-event nerves like the jitters before a big presentation or those butterflies before an exam, chronic anxiety never fully leaves. It wakes you up in the middle of the night, causes your stomach to tighten for no reason, and hijacks your thoughts with an endless cycle of "*what-ifs.*"

And if you're witnessing someone close to you struggling with it, you might feel like you're walking on eggshells, not fully understanding what they're going through. It's not always easy to know how to help or even if you can.

But the truth is anxiety isn't just "in your head." It's your mind and body's alarm system, sometimes sounding the alarm even when there's no fire.

But here's the encouraging part: you *can* learn to manage it. It's possible to regain control and find peace, even when it feels like anxiety is always one step ahead.

For the last 25 years, I've walked this path, experiencing both anxiety and depression firsthand. I've tried everything from medication and therapy to meditation and holistic approaches.

While the struggle hasn't disappeared completely, I've learned to manage it and, in some ways, even draw strength from it. And I know, no matter where you are in your journey, there's hope for you too.

Behavioural and Emotional Aspects of Anxiety

Chronic anxiety doesn't just live in your mind; it seeps into your actions, relationships, and daily habits. It's not just about feeling nervous—it's about how those feelings shape how you think, behave, and even perceive the world.

Behavioral Signs:

- Overthinking every decision.
- Avoiding certain situations or people out of fear.
- Procrastinating because you're afraid of making a mistake.
- Double-checking everything, seeking reassurance, or keeping excessively busy to avoid your thoughts.
- Engaging in constant negative self-talk, convincing yourself you're not good enough.
- Assuming the worst possible outcome in every situation.
- Feeling paralyzed by a lack of confidence due to an unknown fear, doubting your abilities even in familiar situations.

Emotional Signs

Anxiety acts like an emotional magnifying glass. Minor setbacks feel like disasters. Small disagreements leave you reeling.

A constant undercurrent of fear lingers, making even simple tasks feel overwhelming.

Irritability, restlessness, and a gnawing sense of dread become constant companions.

These patterns create a vicious cycle: the more anxious you feel, the more your behavior reinforces those feelings, and the harder it becomes to break free.

Since anxiety is deeply tied to behaviors, it can also be untangled and rewired through new behaviors.

And that's where real hope lies.

The Role of Family and Friends

"Sometimes, the greatest gift you can give someone with anxiety is your understanding."

The people around us play a crucial role in our journey with anxiety. Whether it's through a kind word, a listening ear, or simply their presence, family and friends can make all the difference.

Yet, studies reveal that 40% of people with anxiety feel misunderstood by their loved ones. When friends and family take the time to understand anxiety, those feelings of isolation decrease dramatically, and recovery often accelerates.

I vividly remember moments when I desperately wanted to explain what I was feeling but couldn't find the words. *"Why are you so worried? Just relax!"* people would say. Trust me, if I could've flipped a switch to turn my anxiety off, I would've done it in a heartbeat.

What I've learned is that anxiety thrives on misunderstanding and isolation, but it weakens in the presence of patience, empathy, and connection.

Key Insights

1. **Anxiety is often dismissed, making it harder to seek help**

   - Many people, especially in high-pressure environments, assume anxiety is just "normal stress" and don't recognize it as a serious condition.
   - The lack of validation from others can make anxiety even more isolating and difficult to deal with.

2. **Work & career expectations can worsen anxiety**

   - High achievers often tie their self-worth to career success, making setbacks feel devastating.
   - External pressure (family, peers, mentors) can reinforce the fear of failure.

3. **Professional help is a game-changer**

   - Seeing a psychiatrist shifted the author's journey—highlighting the importance of seeking help.
   - Therapy or medical intervention is not a weakness—it's a necessary step for many struggling with anxiety.

4. **Physical symptoms shouldn't be ignored**

   - Anxiety isn't just in the mind—it manifests in sleeplessness, chest tightness, panic attacks, and more.
   - Ignoring early signs can lead to severe nervous breakdowns if not addressed in time.

Reflect and Act

1. How does anxiety affect your professional life? Have you noticed it impacting your productivity, decision-making, or interactions with colleagues?
2. Have you seen a colleague, employee, or loved one struggle with anxiety at work? How did it affect their performance, confidence, or ability to manage stress?
3. Think about specific situations where anxiety has created challenges in your career or someone else's. Did it lead to missed opportunities, workplace conflicts, or burnout?
4. Set a personal intention. If you experience anxiety, what do you hope to gain from this book—better stress management, improved work-life balance, or tools for handling workplace pressure?
5. What is one small change you can make today to reduce anxiety in your professional life or support someone struggling with it? Consider mindfulness techniques, setting boundaries, or offering encouragement to a colleague in need.
6. Take a moment to reflect—understanding anxiety in the workplace is the first step toward creating a healthier, more balanced work life for yourself and those around you.

Let's take the first step together. Whether you're navigating anxiety yourself or supporting someone who is, understanding anxiety in the workplace is the first step toward creating a healthier, more balanced work life for yourself and those around you.

THE SILENT BATTLE: MY STORY OF DEALING WITH CHRONIC ANXIETY

****

CHAPTER 2: THE FOUNDATIONS OF ANXIETY

*"*Childhood should be carefree, playing in the sun; not living a nightmare in the darkness of the soul."*
—Dave Pelzer, A Child Called "It"*

Anxiety doesn't appear overnight. It's often the result of years of conditioning. From childhood fears to teenage pressures, we slowly build patterns of overthinking, self-doubt, and perfectionism.

Looking back, I can now see how the seeds of my anxiety were planted early through small moments that seemed insignificant at the time but shaped how I viewed myself and the world.

Childhood is like the foundation of a house, every brick laid determines how strong or fragile the structure will be. For me, the bricks were a mix of good times and struggles, of laughter with friends and the quiet weight of expectations.

As I look back now, I can see how those early years planted the seeds of what I later came to understand as anxiety.

In 1985, my parents began discussing a transfer to Gwalior, a move that my mother strongly resisted. She loved Indore—its moderate weather, familiar surroundings, and comfort.

But my grandparents had already moved to Gwalior, and my father's work required us to relocate.

As children, we were indifferent to these changes, but in hindsight, this move shaped my life in more ways than I could have imagined.

My first real struggle began with admission into Saint Paul's School, the most prestigious convent school in Gwalior.

While my sister cleared the entrance easily, I was placed on the waitlist. My mother fought for my admission, persistently meeting with teachers and the principal.

Eventually, I got in, but it wasn't the warm welcome one might hope for.

Saint Paul's was an entirely different world—strict discipline, an English-speaking environment, and Aachamma Madam, a no-nonsense teacher who would pinch and beat students for even the smallest mistakes.

My English was weak, and I struggled to keep up, often finding myself on the receiving end of her discipline.

The move from Indore, where I had done well in school, to this harsh and demanding academic environment left me feeling inadequate.

Adding to the challenge was our relocation to a departmental quarter, two kilometers from my grandparents' home. This meant adjusting to a new home, a new school, and a new social setting all at once.

I did make a few friends—Nischal, Avinish, and Deepak Sharma who would remain a significant part of my social circle for years.

To improve my academics, my parents enrolled me in special tuition classes under Aachamma Madam at her home. My Nanaji (maternal grandfather), who had moved in with us, became my daily escort to these tuition sessions.

Though the discipline was grueling, my studies improved, and by the end of Class 4, I had decent marks.

However, something else happened that year that changed my life, I discovered books.

For my 9th birthday, my father gifted me *Fascinating Animals of the World* by Pustak Mahal. That book sparked a love for reading, leading me to order more books from the "World Famous" series, which my Nanaji paid for upon delivery.

This love for reading became my escape, but it also isolated me, pulling me deeper into my own world.

A Shift in Focus

By the time I reached 5th grade, I had somewhat settled into school life. My friendship with the three Sharmas grew stronger, primarily because of our shared tuition sessions. But my parents unexpectedly discontinued the tuition, believing I could manage on my own. This newfound freedom allowed me to play more, but it also meant that I struggled especially in mathematics.

School life revolved around sports, social dynamics, and growing responsibilities. We played cricket across the two divided sections of our class, with one group from Morar and the other from Thatipur. Our games were intense, but we often lost most matches for reasons beyond our control.

I also formed a close friendship with Mohammad, an introverted but kind classmate. We shared lunch, and he remained a steady friend until Class 10.

But, despite these positive aspects, I started taking things too seriously often getting overly emotional about small conflicts. My teacher pointed this out, but I didn't fully understand it at the time.

Unlike history, where tales of civilizations ignited my curiosity, or psychology, where human behaviour captivated me, math felt like a constant struggle. The rigid formulas and absolute answers left little room for exploration, making every mistake feel like a failure. But looking back, it wasn't the subject itself that held me back. It was the lack of guidance.

Without the right support, the numbers blurred together, and my confidence crumbled. Every time I was called to the board, my heart raced, not just from the challenge of solving equations, but from the fear of facing them alone.

As a result, I scored lower than expected in math, which disappointed my parents. By the end of 5th grade, we moved to CP Colony to live with my grandparents, marking yet another transition in my life.

Probably, to cope, I buried myself in books. Reading became my escape, my way of proving at least to myself that I was good at something.

If I couldn't be great at math, I would master everything else. I started reading beyond the syllabus, absorbing history, politics, and philosophy.

It gave me a sense of control, but on second thoughts, I see that it also became an obsession—a way to silence the voice in my head that told me I wasn't enough.

? Clinical psychologists suggest that parents who frequently "rescue" their children from challenges may inadvertently increase their children's anxiety by preventing them from developing coping skills. (11)

? Discussions have highlighted that emotionally immature parents can instill feelings of instability and anxiety in their children, affecting their emotional development. (12)

? Research indicates a positive correlation between academic anxiety and authoritarian, permissive, and uninvolved parenting styles, while an authoritative style correlates negatively. (13)

? A large study across 21 countries found that nearly one in three mental health conditions in adulthood are directly related to an adverse childhood experience. (14)

Looking back, I realize that my fear of making mistakes started in these early years.

Every incorrect answer, every reprimand, every comparison with a 'smarter' student reinforced the belief that I had to be perfect—or I wasn't good enough.

This belief followed me into adulthood, making it hard to take risks, to accept imperfection, and to trust my own instincts.

Key Insights

1. **Anxiety starts early & often goes unnoticed**

   - Many people don't realize that childhood experiences shape lifelong anxiety patterns.
   - The pressure to succeed, social comparisons, and early failures can create a deep-seated fear of

imperfection.

2. **The need for validation fuels anxiety**

   - Many high achievers tie their self-worth to external validation (grades, approval from parents, social acceptance).
   - The fear of disappointing others creates chronic anxiety.

3. **Coping mechanisms form early & can become unhealthy**

   - Many anxious individuals develop coping mechanisms in childhood—overworking, perfectionism, avoidance—without realizing these habits will intensify over time.

4. **Social anxiety often begins in school**

   - Rejection, bullying, or social pressure can plant the seeds of self-doubt and fear of judgment that carry into adulthood.

Reflect and Act

1. Workplace Stress Triggers – What aspects of your job cause the most anxiety? Deadlines, workplace dynamics, leadership expectations, or job security? How do you currently manage them?

2. Patterns of Stress and Coping – Do you notice recurring patterns in how you handle workplace pressure? Are these responses influenced by past experiences from school, family, or early career struggles?

3. Supporting a Colleague or Loved One – Do you know someone at work or in your personal life who struggles with anxiety? How do they cope, and how can you offer meaningful support without overwhelming them?

4. Advice to Your Younger Self – If you could go back in time, what workplace or career advice would you give your younger self to manage stress better?

5. Creating a Healthier Work-Life Balance – What small but effective steps can you take to reduce anxiety in your daily work routine? Are there habits, boundaries, or mindset shifts that could help?

6. Recognizing Burnout – Have you or someone you know ever reached the point of burnout? What were the warning signs, and what lessons can be learned to prevent it from happening again?

7. Take time to reflect—understanding your patterns and those of people around you can help create a more balanced, supportive, and anxiety-aware work environment.

Understanding where anxiety begins is the first step to managing it. Whether you're facing it yourself or supporting someone who is, awareness and reflection are key.

****

Chapter 3: Shadows in the Hallways

"I remember from my school days Archimedes jumping into his bath and displacing water and coming up with his famous principle, and of course Isaac Newton being hit on the head with an apple. In other words, this realm of human knowledge - which is mathematical, essentially - can have a playful visual element to it."

- James Marsh

The school years are often regarded as a time of innocence and growth, but for me, they carried a quiet undercurrent of anxiety that intertwined with the joys of childhood. Between ages 4 to 9, life was simpler. School was about basic learning, forming friendships, and the excitement of small victories.

But as I stepped into the next stage, from 9 to 12, the challenges of adolescence began to unfold, setting the stage for struggles that would shape my identity.

When we moved to CP Colony, it marked a significant change. The colony itself was a melting pot of backgrounds. A mix of urban sensibilities and rural traditions.

As kids, we played together, unmindful of societal differences. But I could sense the undercurrent of disparity. The boys from rural families carried a roughness that, though unfamiliar, taught me early on about the diversity of human experiences.

By 7th grade, I had established a reputation among teachers and peers as a capable and likable student. My academic performance was commendable, and my circle of friends had expanded. Yet beneath the surface, struggles were brewing.

My parents decided that I no longer needed tuition for math, reasoning that I should be able to manage independently. It wasn't a financial decision but a leap of faith in my capabilities.

Unfortunately, math didn't come easily to me. As the subject grew more complex, the pressure to excel mounted. My struggles with math became a source of personal frustration and societal shame. Success in math was often seen as a measure of intelligence. My appeals to my parents to reinstate tuition were denied, leaving me to wrestle with equations and self-doubt.

During my 10th and 11th grade years, I attended RSS shakhas (branch meetings), primarily due to my grandfather's strong belief in the organization. At that age, ideology held little weight for me.

The Ram Janmabhoomi movement and the prevailing political climate felt distant and abstract. My primary concern was the discomfort I felt wearing the traditional *nikkar* (half trousers). It felt awkward, unattractive, and a constant reminder of my sense of not belonging.

The shakha (branch/unit) meetings consisted of physical exercises, drills, and ideological discussions. While some friends seemed genuinely invested, I struggled to connect with the proceedings. The atmosphere felt overly political, and I couldn't relate to the core messages or the rigid routines.

The political nuances of the discussions often eluded me, and the concept of blindly adhering to an ideology clashed with my naturally inquisitive nature. Eventually, I quietly left the shakha for now.

Later, after detailed research and spending time with left and ultra-left ideologies, I gained a broader perspective on political and social thought. This exploration led me to rejoin the RSS in Bharat, reaffirming my beliefs while appreciating diverse viewpoints.

Social Boycott

Adolescence brought another layer of complexity, an awakening interest in friendships and attraction to the opposite gender. Our conversations shifted from comics to "Hot Wave" T-shirts, hairstyles, and trends. Amid these changes, one girl in my class became the focal point of attention for many, including me.

Our friendship, though innocent, became the center of a controversy. When an anonymous prank call was made to her house, her furious parents assumed the worst.

As fate would have it, I was visiting her home with a group of friends when her mother confronted us. The situation escalated into a full-blown accusation, and the fallout was swift and brutal.

The next day at school, whispers turned into a storm. We were ostracized by both the "good kids" and the so-called "bad boys." Even those I considered close friends abandoned me. My parents, assuming the worst, believed the accusations.

The isolation was crushing. For the first time, I experienced the sharp pain of social rejection—a feeling of being seen as guilty without a chance to defend myself.

With my reputation in tatters, I withdrew from the world and sought refuge in books. What started as a simple escape soon became a coping mechanism one that allowed me to momentarily silence my anxieties and drown out the pressure I felt as the eldest sibling.

There was an unspoken expectation to be a role model, to lead by example, yet inside, I felt anything but strong. As the weight of these expectations grew, so did my obsession with reading. Books weren't just a distraction; they became my shield, my escape, and eventually, an all-consuming fixation that shaped the way I navigated my struggles.

Adapting to Struggles and Learning Resilience

In spite of the confusion, I clung to small routines that provided a semblance of control. Inspired by my grandfather's discipline, I adopted the habit of waking up at 4 AM to study.

In those quiet early hours, when the world was still asleep, I found a temporary escape from the isolation that weighed on me. It was a time when my thoughts were clear, unclouded by the fear of judgment or failure.

But beyond academics, books became my true refuge. The loneliness of struggling to fit in pushed me deeper into reading, and soon, it became more than a pastime. It became an obsession. I devoured almost every book from Pustak Mahal, immersing myself in worlds where language was no barrier and belonging wasn't a struggle.

My academic strengths in subjects like science and Hindi offered a counterbalance to my struggles in math. I leaned into these areas, finding encouragement in the recognition of my teachers. These moments of success reminded me that my worth wasn't solely defined by the challenges I faced, but also by the knowledge and stories I absorbed in solitude.

The books I read became more than just entertainment. They were lifelines that expanded my world, teaching me about resilience, perspective, and the lives of others who overcame challenges. Through them, I discovered a quiet strength within myself, one that helped me navigate the loneliness and rejection I faced.

Maladaptive Coping: Isolation and Rebellion

Not all coping mechanisms were positive. The ostracization at school pushed me further into the margins. With nowhere to belong, I began to associate more with the "bad boys" group. While I didn't fully identify with them, I found a semblance of acceptance that I craved.

At home, the mounting financial pressures and my father's transfer to a rural plant added tension to our household. My mother's stress was palpable, and I often felt helpless, unable to lighten the burden.

My academic struggles and social rejection seemed insignificant compared to the challenges my parents faced, but they left an indelible mark on my psyche.

By 8th grade, the pressure to excel academically intensified. Teachers focused heavily on preparing students for the critical 10th-grade board exams. The competition among classmates was fierce, not just in academics but also in seeking attention and approval. My inability to join a tuition class for math further widened the gap between me and my peers.

The rejection from my former friends, especially the Sharmas, was a wound that refused to heal. I confronted them, questioned their reasons, and even sought support from teachers, but the damage had been done. I became hyper-aware of every action, fearful of making another mistake that would further isolate me.

It was during these years that I began to experience physical manifestations of anxiety—palpitations, a heavy chest, and a constant sense of dread. The weight of expectations, the social rejection, and the internalized pressure to prove myself became overwhelming.

Yet, within these struggles lay the beginnings of resilience. Despite the challenges, I passed 8th grade and moved forward. Many of my peers in the "bad boys" group didn't.

Growth Through Adversity

The school years taught me lessons that extended far beyond the classroom. Rejection, though painful, is not the end—it's a moment that can shape you, but only if you allow it. I experienced firsthand how being different, whether in language skills or social confidence, could make you a target.

I faced the sting of being left out, the whispered conversations that ended when I walked by, and the unspoken rules of social circles I couldn't quite break into.

Bullying wasn't always loud or obvious; sometimes, it was the quiet exclusion that hurt the most. The moments when classmates ignored my presence, when my words felt like they went unheard, and when the fear of humiliation kept me from speaking up.

These experiences made me hyper-aware of how easily a child can internalize feelings of unworthiness. Looking back, I realize how crucial it is to watch children for signs of rejection, not just in the obvious ways, but in the loneliness, they might not even know how to express.

The struggles with math, the silent social boycott, and the tension at home were all pieces of a larger puzzle. They reinforced my fears but also planted the earliest seeds of resilience.

Life's challenges, I began to understand, are not meant to break us but to prepare us to build the strength we will one day need to face even greater battles.

In the next chapter, we'll explore how these formative experiences laid the foundation for the anxiety that would later surface in adulthood and the coping mechanisms, both good and bad, that became a part of my journey.

Key Insights

1. **Anxiety in school isn't just about grades—it's about social survival.**

   - The fear of failure isn't limited to tests—it extends to friendships, interactions, and just existing in school life.

2. **Even in a crowd, anxiety makes you feel alone.**

   - The contrast between being surrounded by people yet feeling isolated is a crucial theme to highlight.

3. **Coping strategies don't always look like coping.**

   - Avoidance, immersing in books, or withdrawing socially may seem like personality traits—but they are often ways of dealing with anxiety.

Reflect and Act

1. Recognizing Early Stress Patterns – Think back to your school years. Were you ever made to feel like you had to prove your worth—through grades, achievements, or social acceptance? How do those experiences influence how you handle pressure at work today?
2. Coping Mechanisms: Helpful or Harmful? – Did you develop certain habits (such as overworking, perfectionism, avoiding conflict, or self-isolation) as a way to cope with childhood stress? Are these habits still serving you well, or are they contributing to burnout and anxiety?
3. Fear of Rejection and Workplace Dynamics – If you experienced exclusion or social anxiety as a child, does that affect your confidence in professional settings? Do you find yourself hesitating to speak up in meetings, struggling with imposter syndrome, or feeling overly

sensitive to criticism?

4. Work-Life Balance and Unspoken Expectations – Many of us internalize the belief that we must always be productive to be valued. Did childhood expectations—such as being the "responsible one" or handling pressure without showing vulnerability—carry over into your adult life? Are they affecting your ability to set boundaries and prioritize your well-being?

5. Supporting Others with Anxiety – If you know someone at work or in your personal life who struggles with chronic anxiety, how can you offer support? Reflect on whether their struggles mirror some of your own experiences and what you can do to foster a more understanding and compassionate environment.

Understanding how early-life stressors influence our present-day behaviors can help us break patterns that no longer serve us. By acknowledging these connections, we can cultivate resilience, set healthier boundaries, and build a work-life balance that prioritizes both success and well-being.

Inner Child Healing

Inner child healing is a process of acknowledging and addressing the emotional needs and wounds of the "inner child," the part of you that was a child, often stemming from experiences in childhood that may have led to unmet needs or unresolved trauma.

Executives, professionals, and high achievers often operate in high-pressure environments that demand confidence, decisiveness, and resilience. Yet, many struggle with anxiety, perfectionism, imposter syndrome, or work-life imbalance—patterns that may be deeply rooted in unresolved childhood experiences. Inner child healing is not just a psychological exercise; it's a transformative process that can help professionals break free from subconscious fears and lead with greater clarity, confidence, and emotional well-being.

Techniques for inner child healing

- Self-compassion: Treat yourself with the same kindness and understanding that you would give to a loved one.
- Write a letter: Write a letter to your inner child, sharing insights from your adult perspective.
- Embrace your emotions: Sit with your emotions, rather than trying to push them away.
- Meditation: Learn to sit with difficult emotions and develop emotional regulation skills.
- Self-reflection: Take time to reflect on your thoughts and actions, and explore the motivations behind them.
- Creative visualization: Imagine yourself as a child and engage in conversations with your inner child.

****

Chapter 4: Navigating College and Independence

""My college experience was like everyone else's. I learned a lot. I gained a new perspective on the world and on people that I'm so thankful and appreciative for."

- Kyle Carpenter"

The transition from high school to college is often painted as an exciting leap toward independence, but for me, it felt more like stepping into a vast and uncharted wilderness. It was 1995, and the air was thick with a singular expectation: pursue engineering or medicine.

Society, peers, and even well-meaning family members reinforced this path as the ultimate measure of success.

At Saint Paul's and Air Force Vidya Bharti, the frenzy was palpable. Almost everyone around me was chasing spots in engineering programs, with many preparing for competitive exams like IIT-JEE or enrolling in local institutions such as MITS. It wasn't just a choice. It was a cultural expectation, a badge of honor that determined your worth in the eyes of neighbors, relatives, and even strangers.

But for me, the idea of pursuing engineering felt like being forced into a mold that didn't fit. Math and science never resonated with me.

They weren't just difficult subjects; they felt distant, mechanical, and devoid of the connection I craved in learning. The rigid formulas, the emphasis on absolute correctness, and the constant pressure to perform left me disengaged and anxious.

Unlike humanities, where history, psychology, and literature sparked my curiosity and made me think critically, math felt like an endless struggle, a subject I was expected to master but could never truly relate to.

The insistent pressure to pursue a field I wasn't passionate about only deepened my aversion. I had already begun to associate math with failure, with hours of staring at problems that refused to make sense, and with the quiet shame of falling behind.

Engineering wasn't just another career choice it symbolized everything I struggled with, a path that felt forced rather than chosen.

I knew my heart wasn't in it, yet I couldn't help but feel the weight of judgment for not following the well-trodden path.

During this time, Bachelor's in Business Administration (BBA) was emerging as a trendy alternative—a course that promised an exciting blend of business knowledge and career prospects.

The buzz around it was electric, but so were the financial barriers. Private colleges offering BBA programs demanded hefty donations ranging from ₹1 lakh to ₹2 lakhs, an astronomical sum for a middle-class family like mine.

I knew my parents wouldn't consider spending such an amount on a course that wasn't as prestigious as engineering or medicine. The societal expectation was clear. Real success lay in technical or medical fields, not in subjects like history or social sciences, which had always fascinated me.

I was drawn to the stories of civilizations, the dynamics of human behaviour, and the way societies evolved over time. But in my world, these interests were seen as hobbies, not viable career paths.

After weeks of deliberation, I opted for a Bachelor of Commerce (B.Com.) at a local college in Morar. The decision was pragmatic: it was affordable, aligned with my long-term goal of pursuing an MBA, and kept me close to home.

But while it made sense on paper, it came with a heavy emotional cost. I couldn't shake the feeling that I was choosing the acceptable path over the one I truly wanted.

The weight of unspoken dreams lingered, reminding me that sometimes, practicality comes at the expense of passion.

The friendships I had cultivated over years at school began to unravel almost overnight. Most of my school friends had chosen engineering, scattering to far-off states or enrolling in prestigious institutions.

They flaunted their motorcycles, shared stories of their vibrant college campuses, and bonded over the shared experience of being engineering students.

I, on the other hand, was left navigating a starkly different reality. The local college I attended lacked the vibrancy I had imagined college life to hold. My classmates were mostly people I hadn't known in school, and while some were friendly, I couldn't shake the feeling of being an outsider.

The conversations around me were different, the ambitions felt more subdued, and I struggled to find a sense of belonging.

My weekends became solitary affairs, spent mostly at home while my former friends posted about group rides and adventures. Invitations to gatherings grew fewer, and eventually, I stopped expecting them altogether. I found myself retreating into a shell, avoiding conversations about college or my choice of course, afraid of the judgment that often followed.

Choosing anything outside engineering or medicine was seen as "settling." Relatives would ask prying questions:

- *"Why didn't you go for engineering like the others?"*
- *"Is B. Com all you could get?"*
- *"What kind of job will you even get with this degree?"*

Even well-meaning acquaintances couldn't hide their disappointment, often offering unsolicited advice about how it wasn't too late to switch to engineering.

Each interaction chipped away at my confidence, reinforcing a sense of inadequacy. I began to dread family gatherings, where these conversations seemed inescapable.

In the isolation, there were moments of unexpected camaraderie. I remember meeting a senior in the college library who had also chosen B.Com. after facing similar societal pressures. We bonded over shared frustrations—how every step outside the "prestigious" fields seemed to come with a need for justification.

Still, loneliness became a constant companion during those years. The isolation, while painful, also gave me the space to reflect on who I was and what I truly wanted.

Without the distractions of a bustling social life, I poured my energy into academics and began exploring subjects that interested me deeply. I spent hours in the library, discovering a love for economics and marketing, and slowly started to build a sense of purpose.

Looking back, those moments of solitude were a double-edged sword. They taught me resilience and self-reliance, but they also left scars of self-doubt that took years to heal. I often wondered how different my college experience might have been if I had chosen engineering not because I wanted to, but because it would have spared me the judgment and loncliness.

What I eventually realized was that stepping into the unknown takes courage, especially when it means going against the tide. Choosing B.Com. wasn't just about picking a course; it was about asserting my individuality in a world that valued conformity.

It was the first step toward carving a path that felt authentic to me, even if it meant enduring years of misunderstanding and isolation.

For anyone reading this who feels trapped by societal expectations, know this: your worth isn't determined by your choice of degree or career. It's shaped by your ability to persevere, to stay true to yourself, and to find meaning in your own journey.

The path may be lonely at times, but it's in those moments of solitude that you discover the strength to keep moving forward.

The New Circle

College ushered me into a new social circle, one that couldn't have been more different from the friendships I had cherished during my school years. These were local boys, many of them from semi-rural backgrounds, whose lives revolved around simple pleasures and unpretentious pursuits.

Their friendship was raw and unpolished but undeniably real. For someone like me, juggling inner turmoil and external expectations, their grounded nature initially felt like a breath of fresh air.

Among them was Maharaj ji, a Muslim boy whose nickname no one ever questioned. Maharaj ji's infectious humour and earthy wisdom often served as a balm to my overthinking tendencies. His presence had a way of grounding the group, turning even the most mundane moments into something memorable.

He quickly became a central figure in my new life, offering companionship that felt uncomplicated compared to the strained relationships I had left behind.

Despite their friendship, I couldn't ignore how out of place I felt. These boys had grown up in a different world, shaped by rural life and a culture of close-knit communities. Their discussions revolved around local gossip, family dramas, and traditions I couldn't entirely relate to.

Their aspirations were modest, often centered around securing stable government jobs or continuing family businesses.

In contrast, I was preoccupied with thoughts of pursuing an MBA and breaking into the corporate world dreams that felt distant and perhaps even foreign in their context.

While they lived in the present, I was haunted by the future.

The differences weren't just intellectual but cultural, leaving me feeling like I straddled two very different worlds.

This contrast often led to a sense of emotional disconnection. While I appreciated their authenticity, I struggled to align my own identity with the group. It felt as though I was borrowing their companionship rather than truly belonging.

One evening, Maharaj ji suggested a ride on my recently restored 1978 Yezdi Classic motorcycle. The bike had become a personal project and a symbol of individuality after I refurbished it with funds from my nanaji (grandfather).

That night, we rode through the winding roads leading to Gwalior Fort. As the city lights sparkled below us, Maharaj ji leaned against the bike and said, *"Yaar, life is simple. Stop overthinking and take one thing at a time."*

His advice was deceptively simple but deeply resonant. For a moment, it felt like the weight on my chest had eased. But these moments of relief were fleeting. The very simplicity of their lives, which I admired, also reminded me of my own restlessness.

Their interests—like the local akharas, wrestling, or intense bodybuilding regimens often highlighted my insecurities. At first, I joined them in the akhara (traditional Indian wrestling training centre), eager to immerse myself in their world. But my clumsy attempts at wrestling only underscored my limitations. Where they found camaraderie and strength, I found frustration and self-doubt.

Even as I tried to integrate into this new circle, I felt the sharp edges of isolation. I couldn't talk to them about the things that kept me awake at night: the societal pressure to succeed, the lingering sense of failure, or the relentless judgments I faced at home.

Conversations remained light, focused on local events or playful teasing. My internal struggles were mine alone to bear.

This sense of detachment mirrored what I felt with my old friends from school. When we met during holidays, the conversations that once flowed naturally now felt stiff and awkward. They spoke about their engineering colleges, coding competitions, and the thrill of cracking technical challenges.

Meanwhile, my stories about college life seemed trivial in comparison.

As I listened to them recount their adventures, I couldn't help but feel left behind, not just in terms of career paths but in the very rhythm of life. They were sprinting ahead in a race I wasn't even sure I wanted to join.

The isolation wasn't confined to my social circles. At home, the weight of my parents' disapproval loomed large. My father, a man of practicality and ambition, viewed my decision to pursue B.Com. as a missed opportunity. To him, engineering was the path to respectability and success, and anything else felt like settling.

Conversations with my extended family only deepened this sense of inadequacy. Every gathering became an inquisition, filled with probing questions:

- *"What's the plan after B.Com.? Are you even considering an MBA?"*
- *"Why didn't you aim for CA or something more serious?"*
- *"Do you think this degree is enough to support a family in the future?"*

Their remarks weren't outright hostile, but the undertone of disappointment was impossible to ignore. I often left these gatherings feeling small, my choices weighed down by their collective judgment.

Even my Yezdi, once a symbol of freedom, began to feel like an ironic contradiction. It was my attempt to assert independence, yet every ride seemed to bring me closer to the realization of how tightly bound I was by societal and familial expectations.

In many ways, I was living in a no-man's land. With my new circle of friends, I was the ambitious outsider. With my old friends, I was the underachiever. At home, I was the dutiful son who couldn't quite measure up to the dreams his parents had for him.

This divided personality feeling neither here nor there became a defining feature of those college years. I tried to compartmentalize my life, but the emotional toll was undeniable. There were days when I withdrew entirely, finding solace in books or late-night rides on my Yezdi. Even those escapes, however, felt temporary, like bandages on a wound that refused to heal.

Amid this tug-of-war, there were moments of clarity that offered hope. One evening, after a particularly gruelling day, Maharaj ji sat me down and said, "Stop trying to fit in everywhere. You're different, and that's okay. You'll find your way."

His words, simple as they were, planted a seed. Perhaps belonging didn't mean blending in. Perhaps it meant carving out a space where I could be myself, unburdened by expectations and judgments.

To support myself, I started offering tuition classes, beginning with my friends' younger siblings. As word spread, more students came my way, and before long, I had a steady stream of learners, earning around ₹2,000 to ₹3,000 per month.

This income not only helped fund my studies but also allowed me to maintain my Yezdi and enjoy life's little luxuries—occasional dining out and, most importantly, never missing a Govinda movie. His effortless dance moves and infectious energy were a welcome escape, adding a spark of joy to my otherwise routine life.

The First Signs of Breaking

The cracks began to show during my second year of B.Com. By then, the conflicting worlds I got on—my new circle of friends, the lingering memories of old friendships, and the constant judgment at home had created an emotional weight that I carried everywhere.

The pressure to meet expectations, fit in, and carve out a sense of identity had quietly built to a breaking point.

One morning, I woke up with an unfamiliar heaviness. The comforting rhythm of daily life—the chirping birds, the street vendors calling out their wares felt distant, almost unreal.

A tightness gripped my chest, and an overwhelming fatigue pinned me to my bed.

The thoughts came like waves, relentless and suffocating:

- *"You're falling behind."*
- *"You'll never achieve anything significant."*
- *"What's the point of all this effort?"*

By the time I managed to leave the house and make it to class, I felt like a hollow version of myself. My body was there, but my mind was trapped in a downward spiral of doubt and dread.

That day in class, I sat quietly, barely registering the lecture. My chest felt like it was being squeezed, and each breath was a conscious effort. My friends noticed my change in behavior and tried to cheer me up with jokes and casual witty remarks, but their efforts only deepened my sense of isolation.

I couldn't bring myself to explain what I was feeling—not to them, not to my parents, not even to myself. How do you describe a weight that feels both invisible and unbearable? I smiled faintly, nodded at the right moments, and went through the motions, all the while feeling like I was cracking inside.

In hindsight, the breakdown didn't come out of nowhere. It was the peak of years of affected pressure:

- The expectations to follow a path I didn't want.
- The divide between the grounded simplicity of my new friends and the ambitious futures of my old ones.

I had spent so much time trying to juggle these competing realities that I hadn't noticed the toll it was taking on my mental health. The nights of overthinking, the days of feeling inadequate, and the ever-present fear of failure had built up like water behind a dam. That morning, the dam cracked.

Looking back, that first breakdown was a quiet alarm bell, a signal that something within me needed attention. At the time, I didn't recognize it for what it was. I saw it as a weakness, a personal failing. But in reality, it was my mind and body's way of saying, "Slow down. Pay attention."

That episode marked the beginning of a struggle I would come to know intimately: the cycle of anxiety, isolation, and self-doubt. It wasn't the last time I would feel that way, but it was the first time I realized just how fragile I had become.

Crossroads

The path I'd chosen felt increasingly uncertain. The casual ridicule from my less intellectually inclined friends, coupled with a growing sense of alienation from the engineering-focused crowd, chipped away at my confidence. The pain, though internalized, was real. Doubt bit me. Had I made the wrong decision?

The constant buzz about the lucrative salaries engineering graduates were commanding only intensified these anxieties. Was I missing out on something significant? Yet, a quiet voice within me insisted that engineering wasn't my calling. The bus had left, and I wasn't on it. Accepting that, however, was a daily struggle. These thoughts often became a heavy burden, plunging me into spirals of self-doubt.

In this confusion, a fascination with politics blossomed. I devoured magazines, watched countless TV shows, and even engaged in role-playing, arguing both sides of the political spectrum. This burgeoning passion led me to debate competitions, a platform where I honed my argumentative skills and even earned a few accolades.

Growing up in a family with right-leaning political views, my initial leanings were naturally conservative. However, college became a period of ideological exploration, a brief flirtation with the left as I sought understanding and a sense of belonging.

The political climate was volatile. The BJP's short-lived 13-day coalition government had come and gone. During this period, large RSS gatherings in Gwalior were frequent, and I attended several *Baudhiks* (intellectual discussions). I even had the opportunity to hear RSS Chief K.S. Sudarshan speak – a memorable experience. The subsequent fall of the BJP government, however, brought a wave of disappointment, mirroring the disillusionment felt by many in our circle.

Meanwhile, the nagging neck pain persisted, a physical manifestation of the emotional and mental stress I was under. Despite the discomfort, my tuition work provided a steady income, which I primarily spent on books, meals out, and maintaining my beloved Yezdi motorcycle.

This became my routine: balancing work, studies, and these small indulgences to maintain some semblance of equilibrium.

My second year concluded with decent grades, though not as high as I had hoped. In a moment of frustration, I applied for revaluation in two subjects, but the results remained unchanged. It was a stark reminder that while I was moving forward, the journey was far from easy.

The pressure intensified during my third year of B.Com. The combined weight of family expectations and societal judgment became almost unbearable. I began withdrawing from family gatherings, even skipping my cousin's wedding.

The whispers and sideways glances about my choice to pursue B.Com. instead of the more "prestigious" engineering path were relentless. It felt easier to avoid these events altogether than to endure the judgment and condescension.

My intellectual curiosity, fuelled by constant reading, found no outlet. My circle of friends, who didn't share my intellectual interests, often ridiculed my pursuits, further isolating me.

Around this time, I met my first self-proclaimed Communist, a local *paanwala* (betel leaf seller) who had set up shop in our neighbourhood. He was a fascinating character, always eager to share propaganda—small, pocket-sized booklets filled with leftist ideology.

It soon became clear that he was likely a full-time Communist party worker.

His shop became a venue for lively debates. He would passionately explain his views and offer me literature, which I diligently read, intrigued by the stark contrast to the political ideologies I'd grown up with. These exchanges were my first real engagement with leftist thought, and I was impressed by its consistency and enthusiasm.

Then, as suddenly as they began, our discussions ceased. One day, the *paanwala* was gone, his shop shuttered without explanation.

His abrupt disappearance left me pondering the complexities of ideological conviction, and this brief encounter with Communist thought added another layer to my evolving worldview.

The Road to MBA

As my B.Com. years drew to a close, the next logical step was preparing for the MBA entrance exams, a milestone that felt both promising and daunting. For months, my life revolved around mock tests, late-night study sessions, and the relentless pressure of outperforming my peers. Preparing for the exams provided a sense of structure and purpose, but it also amplified the fears that had quietly been building within me.

As I geared up for my MBA entrance exams, I also started preparing for Bank Probationary Officer exams, recognizing their similarities in structure and content. I wanted to keep my options open anything that could serve as a stepping stone toward financial independence.

Then, one day, during a casual cricket match, fate intervened. I met my friend's boss, a Regional Manager at a mid-sized pharmaceutical company. He was impressed by my spoken English and, out of the blue, asked if I'd be interested in working as a Medical Representative (MR).

I told him I was still in my final year of college, expecting that to be a dealbreaker. But to my surprise, he was unfazed and offered me the job anyway.

That's how I found myself in the pharmaceutical industry, selling bulk drugs and branded formulations. My primary goal was simple: earn enough to fund my MBA.

From casual conversations with medical representative friends during smoke breaks, I had gathered that the job wasn't particularly complicated. By then, I had already picked up smoking and drinking habits that had quietly woven themselves into my routine.

The salary was good, and with incentives, I had the potential to make around ₹10,000 per month, a small fortune for someone with minimal expenses.

Harsh Reality of Pharma Sales

The onboarding process began with classroom training, followed by field training under the guidance of my boss, C.P.S. Raghuvanshi, a seasoned pharmaceutical salesperson. My immediate manager, S.M. Sharma was equally supportive, and their mentorship gave me confidence.

But no amount of training could have prepared me for the reality of the job.

At first, I imagined it would be simple—meet doctors, introduce products, and secure prescriptions. But the moment I stepped into the field, I realized how wrong I was.

Maybe it was just a lack of experience or the uncertainty that comes with being new to something. Every interaction with doctors, pharmacists, and dealers triggered an unsettling mix of hesitation and anxiety.

My heart would race, my mind would go blank, and articulating my thoughts felt like an uphill battle. It was confusing—I had never struggled with communication before, yet in this professional setting, I suddenly found myself second-guessing every word.

Then came the deeper revelations. The pharmaceutical industry was full of malpractices—doctors prescribing medications in exchange for commissions and gifts, diagnostic labs offering kickbacks, and drugs being sold at outrageous markups, often for conditions that didn't even require them.

Patients weren't treated as people; they were revenue streams.

I quickly learned the "game" and adapted. I played along to meet my sales quotas, but the ethical compromises gnawed at me. Each day, I was torn between professional obligations and personal values. The pressure to hit targets was relentless, making it one of the most stressful experiences I had ever endured.

Though the financial rewards were tempting, the job left me feeling hollow. It didn't take long for me to realize this wasn't my future. It was just a means to an end. My real goal remained unchanged: to pursue an MBA and build a career on my own terms.

A Crisis of Confidence

Despite my efforts, there was one consistent piece of feedback from my superiors and clients—I was too serious. Doctors, colleagues, even my bosses noted that I came across as overly formal, maybe even intimidating. In truth, I was struggling with an invisible weight, a constant, inexplicable unease that made every interaction feel like a test I was failing.

There were days when I couldn't explain why I felt this way. The self-doubt, the hesitation, the rigid seriousness—it all formed a cocktail of anxiety that followed me into every conversation.

I did my best to keep up appearances, building enough trust with doctors to hit my targets, but deep down, I knew I was merely surviving, not thriving. To cope, I sought escape.

Gwalior was changing. The city's first discotheque, Euphoria, had just opened, and it quickly became my go-to spot for unwinding.

After long, exhausting days, I would find solace in music, food, and the rare moments of freedom.

Cable TV had arrived too, introducing us to a world of metro city glamour—modelling, nightlife, and modern aspirations. It was fascinating to watch, a stark contrast to the grind of my daily life.

My evenings often revolved around highway dhabas (highway motels), good food, and deep conversations with friends.

These small pleasures became my refuge, a brief respite from the pressures of work and the moral dilemmas I faced.

A Defining Decision

As the MBA entrance exams drew closer, I made a decision that sent shockwaves through my family. I quit my job.

My parents were stunned. In their eyes, I had a stable career with a promising future. They had already started considering marriage prospects, assuming I was settled.

Walking away from a steady paycheck, especially when I had no guarantees about the future, seemed reckless to them.

"You're making a huge mistake," they said.

Even my bosses tried to dissuade me, emphasizing my potential in the industry. They believed I could go far if I stayed. But I knew better. The corruption, the compromises, the emptiness—it wasn't a life I wanted.

I had no intention of spending my career convincing doctors to prescribe unnecessary drugs.

With just two months left for the MBA entrance exams, I took the plunge. I dedicated myself entirely to studying, determined to secure my place in a top program. I had always been drawn to JUMBA. The building itself exuded an aura of academic prestige.

The thought of walking its halls, immersing myself in learning, and finally stepping onto the path I had envisioned for myself filled me with excitement.

My parents remained skeptical, worried about the risks. But I had never been more certain of anything.

I wasn't running away from a job; I was running toward my future.

The MBA Journey Begins

In the year 2000, I sat for the MBA entrance exams, after months of rigorous preparation. My hard work paid off—I secured a high rank, opening doors to some of the top business schools in the state, including the esteemed School of Studies (SOS) in Indore.

The prospect of studying in Indore, a city renowned for its academic excellence and dynamic student culture, was both exciting and deeply compelling.

However, my parents had other plans. Citing various reasons, they decided I wouldn't be leaving town for my MBA. One major factor was their belief that I had become a bit "out of hand", a perception fueled by my growing independence and a few questionable habits I had picked up.

Their concerns were further reinforced by an astrologer's warning that hostel life could be detrimental to me. In their eyes, staying close to home was the safer and more responsible choice.

While I was disappointed, I couldn't ignore my excitement about joining Jiwaji University's Management School of Studies (JUMBA). The JUMBA building had always intrigued me, representing both academic ambition and a fresh start.

I had high hopes for the MBA program—new learning opportunities, personal growth, and the chance to build a career that aligned with my aspirations.

Yet, alongside the anticipation, there was a lingering sense of unease. Leaving my job as a Medical Representative role that had provided financial stability and a structured routine was a daunting decision.

Though demanding, the job had given me a sense of independence, and stepping away from it to fully immerse myself in academics felt like a leap into the unknown.

The early days at JUMBA were a blur of introductions, orientation sessions, and icebreaker activities designed to help us bond as a batch.

My classmates quickly began forming cliques, mostly based on shared schools, regions, or even socioeconomic backgrounds.

The competitive undercurrent was palpable. There was an unspoken race to establish dominance, whether through academic prowess, charisma, or sheer social influence.

I gravitated toward a group of boys from Saint Paul's, my old school. Though we hadn't been close during our school days, their presence provided a show of familiarity in this new environment. But even within this group, I felt the faint echoes of my earlier struggles with fitting in.

Human Resource Management (HRM) was unfamiliar territory for me, so I asked around. Friends described it as a field of higher-level concepts, one that came with influence and authority.

Intrigued, I kept it in mind as a potential choice.

The first semester flew by in a blur of classes, assignments, and a lot of fun.

Our MBA batch naturally split into three distinct groups—one consisting of my friends from Saint Paul's, another made up of boys from across the river, mostly from Carmel Convent, and the third comprising students from outside Gwalior.

Our group, with our reputation for smoking, drinking, and living a little on the edge, was quickly labelled the "rough boys."

Academically, the experience was refreshing. Classes were engaging, filled with lively discussions and real-world case studies.

JUMBA also hosted a grand introduction party, complete with a touch of ragging, but it turned out to be more fun than intimidating.

Those early days brought a rush of excitement, reminding me of the carefree moments I had been missing for a long time.

Academic Awakening and Social Dynamics

In the second semester, we were introduced to all the major specializations, and fortunately, we had some of the best faculty members guiding us. Dr. Namita Roy, a PhD in Psychology, taught Organizational Behaviour (OB) with remarkable insight, while our HRM professor, deep into his PhD in Talent Management, brought a wealth of industry knowledge.

I also discovered that Gwalior had a strong alumni network in HR, with an affiliated college that had been running a PG Diploma in HRM for the past two decades.

JUMBA's library was a treasure trove, and I quickly became engrossed in OB. The psychological aspects of the subject fascinated me. It was like unlocking a new way of understanding people and organizations.

Theories of motivation, leadership development, and group dynamics particularly captivated me. My curiosity soon turned into an obsession; I checked out every OB book I could find, eager to absorb every insight.

My growing interest in HR extended beyond academics. I wanted hands-on experience, so I decided to pursue my summer internship in HR.

The alumni network made securing a placement seamless, and I landed an internship at a major tire company with a large plant in Gwalior.

Over the course of the internship, I worked on two key projects—one focused on the implementation of Total Quality Management (TQM), and the other on conducting a worker motivation survey. The experience cemented my belief in HR's impact on both organizations and society.

Yet, despite my intellectual enthusiasm, I couldn't shake a lingering sense of emptiness. My palpitations persisted, and my anxieties grew.

At home, communication had dwindled to almost nothing over the past few years, deepening my isolation.

Ironically, the more I explored psychology, the more I found myself analyzing every interaction—only to feel even more alone.

I could feel myself slipping into a state of mental exhaustion. Overthinking, relentless analysis, and a complete lack of leisure had trapped me in a vicious cycle of stress.

Even my friends noticed, urging me to take a break, and my professors questioned why I was over analyzing everything.

I had accumulated so much knowledge but lacked an outlet to apply it, leaving me feeling like a ticking time bomb. Instead of seeking relief, I withdrew further into myself, becoming more distant and isolated.

My mind had become a pressure cooker, thoughts and emotions building up, ready to explode at any moment. But amidst this mental turmoil, a new passion began to take shape.

I learned that JUMBA had a strong alumni network, yet the annual fest hadn't been held for five years due to ongoing disputes with university management over funding. I saw an opportunity and took it upon myself to revive the event.

With the arrival of the junior batch, it felt like a fresh start. This was our time to lead, to shape the institution's future, and I was eager to take on the responsibility.

I had already begun establishing myself within the MPM Alumni network, gaining access to their directory and reaching out extensively.

My efforts weren't just about networking—they were driven by a deeper fear: uncertainty about my future job prospects. I knew I couldn't wait for opportunities; I had to create them.

To establish credibility, I wrote several articles for the alumni souvenir, hoping to make an impression. The journey was tough, but my persistence paid off.

After relentless negotiations, I convinced the university management to approve an alumni event under a self-funded model. Organizing it was a massive undertaking, but I was able to rally different student groups to contribute.

However, one major hurdle remained. The university insisted on forming a student body to oversee the event, fearing conflicts among student groups. They weren't wrong. There were at least three or four candidates vying for the position of president, and an election would likely lead to chaos.

Understanding the internal dynamics, I played a strategic psychological game.

I secretly met with the leaders of the two other major groups and pre-decided the distribution of roles. Each group would control a critical part of the event, ensuring no one felt sidelined.

This eliminated the need for an election and kept the planning process smooth and unified.

With that settled, I turned my attention to the juniors. I was determined to pass on everything I had learned about Organizational Behaviour (OB) and Human Resource Management (HR). Leadership theories, motivation, cognitive biases

I discussed them obsessively, eager to share my insights with anyone who would listen.

Amidst all this, I found myself drawn to a girl in the junior batch. Mustering the courage, I confessed my feelings, but she turned me down. Though rejection wasn't new to me, this one stung more than usual. Unwilling to give up, I enlisted her friend, Pragati, as a mediator, hoping to change her mind. In an unexpected twist, Pragati and I grew close, and over time, she became the most important person in my life.

Eventually, we got married—a journey from rejection to love that was both painful and beautiful.

Meanwhile, the alumni event, Magnafest was a resounding success. Our self-funded model exceeded expectations, raising 200% more than our initial targets through sponsorships and advertisements in the event souvenir. The three-day event became one of the largest gatherings the university had ever hosted.

Faculty members were astonished by the scale and organization, and I personally connected with nearly every alumnus, from the very first batch to the most recent graduates.

What made this achievement even more meaningful was that the self-funded model we pioneered continued to sustain Magnafest for the next 5-7 years, setting a lasting precedent. Knowing that our efforts had created a legacy filled me with immense pride.

As the semester progressed, we transitioned into our majors. I chose Marketing and HR, and the coursework became even more engaging. Consumer Behaviour and HRM fascinated me in ways I hadn't anticipated, bringing business dynamics to life in a practical and exciting way.

We were introduced to a new faculty member, Anuj Sir, a 1995 graduate who had held senior HR roles in a major Middle Eastern oil and gas company. His real-world experience and insights made HR and leadership studies even more compelling.

With our third semester coming to an end, we were stepping into the final stretch of our journey. But as graduation loomed closer, so did my fears. The weight of expectations, career decisions, and the uncertainty of the future pressed down on me harder than ever.

As the fourth semester began, life grew heavier—both at home and in college. My father faced an immense challenge at work, forced into early retirement. The news hit us like a storm. In response, he decided to move from Chhattisgarh to Madhya Pradesh, but the abrupt shift, coupled with the uncertainty surrounding his retirement plan, left our family in turmoil. The weight of it all bore down on me, and my thoughts spiraled into an unrelenting cycle of negativity.

Mornings became the hardest. My mind raced, my heart pounded, and no matter how much I tried to push through, the anxiety felt suffocating. I sought refuge in books and writing, losing myself in Rediff's discussion boards as a distraction.

Faculty and alumni reassured me that things would eventually work out, but their words did little to quiet the storm inside me.

The Breakdown

Then came March, the turning point. My father's retirement was finalized, and the shock was crippling. Our home, still under construction, became an added source of stress. Worse, his retirement wasn't voluntary; it was forced and illegal.

Determined to fight, he filed a case, a battle that would stretch over ten years, reaching all the way to the Supreme Court before he ultimately won. But in that moment, all we felt was devastation.

Watching my father, once a pillar of strength, stripped of his position and grappling with helplessness was unbearable. I had always looked up to him, yet now, I saw him vulnerable for the first time. My worries deepened. In 2001, the job market was already suffering due to a recession, and every news headline only fuelled my anxiety.

A professor, noticing my growing distress, suggested I see a psychologist. She had been observing me for a while and genuinely cared. Taking her advice, I met with a counsellor. The sessions provided some relief, but they weren't enough. My struggles persisted.

Some days, I felt normal and even confident. But all it took was a small trigger, a thought, an event, or sometimes nothing at all to send me plunging into darkness.

The negativity morphed into self-loathing, and my fear of leaving Gwalior, compounded by the rejection from the girl I had feelings for, only added to the weight. Everything seemed to be unravelling, and I felt trapped inside my own mind.

On the surface, I appeared fine. I was functioning. But inside, I was drowning. I couldn't put into words the darkness consuming me, and I feared no one would understand. Slowly, my thoughts took a darker turn, edging toward suicidal territory.

I knew these feelings were wrong, but I couldn't stop them. Sleepless nights only made things worse, leaving me mentally and physically drained.

Desperate, I reached out to Dr. Sharma, the father of my friend Deepak. The moment he saw me, he recognized the severity of my condition and immediately referred me to Dr. Gupta, a psychiatrist. Sensing my fragile state, Deepak offered to drive me to the appointment and take me home afterward.

That evening, Dr. Gupta saw me well past his usual hours. He listened patiently, without interruption, his empathy offering a rare sense of relief. After our conversation, he prescribed antidepressants and sedatives to help manage my anxiety and exhaustion.

His instructions were clear: stop reading the news, focus only on my exams, and have an open conversation with my parents.

The next two weeks were gruelling. My exams loomed, and though I had prepared well, the anxiety was relentless. I lost weight, my confidence eroded, and my emotional turmoil became visible to those around me. Every day felt like a battle.

And then, something unexpected happened. Pragati, a close friend who had been acting as a mediator between me and the girl I liked, confessed her feelings for me. Despite my inner chaos, she saw something in me. In that moment, amidst all the uncertainty, I found a glimmer of hope.

Perhaps, after all the pain and fear, a new chapter was waiting for me.

Looking back, my MBA experience was a study in contrasts: the intellectual clarity of OB classes versus the emotional chaos of campus life; the competitiveness of group dynamics versus the quiet solace of my moments with Pragati.

The lessons I learned weren't confined to textbooks or lectures.

They came from navigating rejection, finding unexpected connections, and learning to reconcile the different parts of myself, the ambitious student, the anxious dreamer, and the person who just wanted to belong.

Key Insights

1. Independence is both liberating & terrifying

- The shift from structured school life to the unpredictability of college brings both freedom and anxiety.
- The fear of making wrong choices, losing old friendships, and struggling to fit into a new world are universal themes.

2. **The weight of societal expectations never really goes away**

   ◦ The pressure to follow a "prestigious" career path lingers, even when a personal choice (MBA) is made.
   ◦ Anxiety isn't just about failing—it's about being judged for making a different choice.

3. **Anxiety in college looks different but still stays**

   ◦ Unlike school, where anxiety came from academic pressure, college anxiety is more about uncertainty, identity, and social belonging.

4. **Coping mechanisms start forming, even if we don't recognize them**

   ◦ Books, tuition classes, side hustles, political engagement, and overworking—all became ways to manage stress and gain control.

Reflect and Act

1. Think back to a time when work-related stress or anxiety affected your performance. How did you cope, and what did you learn from the experience?
2. Consider a colleague, friend, or family member who struggles with anxiety. How have you supported them, and what more can you do to help them feel understood?

3. Write an affirmation or encouraging statement that could help you or someone you know during a stressful moment at work. How can you remind yourself of this in high-pressure situations?
4. Identify a coping strategy that helps you manage workplace anxiety today. How can you refine or expand on this approach to build long-term resilience?
5. Think about your work-life balance. Are you prioritizing self-care, or are stress and expectations taking a toll on your well-being? What small change can you make to create a healthier balance?

Self-reflection is key to recognizing patterns, setting boundaries, and developing healthier ways to navigate anxiety—for yourself and those around you.

****

CHAPTER 5. BALANCING ACTS: WORK, MARRIAGE, AND THE WEIGHT OF EXPECTATIONS

""We love to expect, and when expectation is either disappointed or gratified, we want to be again expecting."

- Samuel Johnson "

Once I completed my MBA, I was so disheartened, depressed, and anxious that I even considered pursuing a PhD or becoming a professor at a local college. When an offer for an assistant professor position at a private college in Gwalior came my way, I seriously considered it, thinking academia might provide the stability and purpose I was struggling to find.

However, I moved to Delhi for job hunting. Once in Delhi, I turned to our alumni network for support, sharing my situation and seeking job opportunities. The response was incredible.

Within a week, I received two offers: one for the assistant professor position and another from a top IT company in their recruiting department.

Both opportunities came through alumni connections, a testament to the dedication I had poured into Magnafest and alumni events.

Just as I was debating which path to take, Abhishek, my MBA batch mate, stepped in with an offer of free accommodation, making the transition to Delhi much easier.

With his support and the unexpected generosity of my network, I finally felt like things were beginning to fall into place.

Finding My Footing in the Corporate World

I landed a position with a leading IT services company in the recruiting function, thanks to a valuable connection through an alumnus. The recruiting department had a specialized head hunters' group focused on mapping talent across designated territories.

At that time, job boards like Naukri.com and Monster.com were still in their infancy, so headhunting mainly relied on cold calling and generating leads during personal interviews. My boss, a senior executive from the 1996 batch, played a key role in shaping my early experiences.

In the first few weeks, I was tasked with observing and assisting in interviews and weekend hiring drives. It was an enjoyable experience, but not exactly what I had envisioned.

I had anticipated working in Organizational Behaviour (OB) and talent management, not recruitment. In college, recruitment was often regarded as a clerical function, and I struggled to shake off that perception.

Commuting to the office was another challenge, particularly in the evenings. If I missed the last bus at 7:30 PM, the journey back home became a daunting task. As a result, I always aimed to leave before that time.

After a few weeks of observation, I was given the responsibility of headhunting. I shadowed a senior headhunter and quickly found the process fascinating.

With my natural ability to make prank and cold calls, I adapted well.

Our task was to sift through databases, reach out to potential candidates, and generate leads, often through cold calls to office board lines.

I closely observed my senior colleagues, took diligent notes, and soon became proficient in headhunting and talent mapping. This experience became the foundation for my professional growth.

Despite the high-pressure environment and the constant vigilance of target companies, I found the work to be incredibly rewarding.

The company was a dream employer for many, and the free breakfast, lunch, and evening snacks were a welcome relief, especially considering the high cost of eating out.

As I gained confidence and became a top performer in headhunting, I began to realize the broader psychological aspects of the role, which I found particularly intriguing.

However, the work was taxing, especially when dealing with niche skill sets that were in limited supply. Late-night calls were common, as candidates often preferred to speak after office hours.

Although I enjoyed the work, my chronic anxiety remained a challenge. Despite being on antidepressants, I began to experience noticeable side effects, particularly weight gain.

My boss, though supportive in some ways, was also a tough taskmaster. His harsh words during moments of anger triggered severe anxiety attacks, leaving me feeling worthless and overwhelmed with despair.

These moments often sent me into tears, struggling to manage the crushing weight of self-doubt.

To cope with these intense episodes, I developed a simple but effective mechanism. Whenever a panic attack struck, I would take a break, call a friend, or head to the canteen for a small indulgence. This brief escape helped me break the chain of negative thoughts and provided a much-needed respite.

A senior colleague offered some wisdom that struck a chord: "*Corporate life has its share of politics and hurdles, but consistent, sincere work will eventually be rewarded.*" His words sparked a period of deep self-reflection.

I recognized that certain habits were not only unproductive but were actively contributing to my rising anxiety levels.

One of the first things I did was take a break from reading, particularly the psychology books I'd leaned towards. Ironically, what I'd sought as a source of comfort had become a catalyst for overthinking. Each page seemed to fuel my spiraling thoughts rather than soothe them.

Simultaneously, I tackled two other damaging habits: smoking and tobacco use. I knew their harmful effects were undeniable, and I made a conscious, determined decision to quit entirely.

What had once felt like a momentary escape from the crushing weight of anxiety had become a burden in itself, impacting both my health and my finances.

I could feel its grip tightening, a constant reminder of my vulnerability.

These seemingly small but significant changes became crucial tools in steering the storm of anxiety.

They allowed me to regain a sense of control, manage my mental well-being, and continue performing effectively at work.

Mid-Career Life: Growth, Challenges, and Self-Discovery

At home, the atmosphere was thick with tension and stress. My father was caught in a lengthy legal battle that cast a long shadow over our daily lives. It was a time marked by uncertainty and emotional upheaval, and the weight of it all often felt unbearable, leaving me weak and vulnerable.

Despite being on medication, the anxiety stayed, and the pills seemed powerless against the relentless waves of dread that gripped me.

During these dark moments, I found solace in my conversations with Pragati. We often connected via messenger and public phones. Her words were a temporary reprieve for my troubled mind.

When I visited Gwalior, she confided that her parents were aggressively searching for a suitable match for her. The urgency in her voice added another layer to my anxiety. I had just started my job, my salary was modest, and the future was a fog of uncertainty.

The thought of not being able to provide for a potential marriage weighed heavily on me.

One evening, while aimlessly browsing the internet, I stumbled upon a Yahoo group dedicated to anxiety relief. Desperate for any kind of hope, I reached out, and soon, volunteers from the group contacted me.

They recommended I join a course called the "Art of Living." At first, I dismissed it as another empty promise, skeptical of its potential. But the volunteers persisted, even offering to cover the cost if I didn't find it helpful. Despite their kind offer, I felt overwhelmed and decided to put the idea aside for the time being.

Financial strain only deepened my worries. I had moved into my own place, but money was tight, and my salary barely covered the basics. I had taken loans from friends like Abhishek, and the pressure of repayment loomed over me.

Adding to this, Pragati's parents' disapproval hung heavily in the air. I knew they would never approve of our marriage given my current financial situation, which made changing my circumstances all the more urgent.

Then, one day, my boss, Amit, shared surprising news that he had resigned from his position and secured a new job in Pune, complete with a significant promotion and pay raise. While I was happy for him, the news left me feeling even more uncertain about my own future.

Amit reassured me, promising to hire me once he was settled, though it might take six to twelve months. His words gave me a ray of hope, but they also highlighted the need for immediate action.

The job I had secured was on a contract basis, offering stability for the time being, but the salary, while decent, was still lower than I had hoped. I knew I couldn't rely solely on future promises I needed to make the most of the present opportunity while keeping an eye out for better prospects.

Determined to improve my situation, I began actively searching for new opportunities, reaching out to my JUMBA alumni network for support. This period of struggle taught me several important lessons:

1. **Identify Unproductive Activities:** I recognized the importance of identifying activities that increased my stress rather than alleviating it. Reading, while educational, often fuelled my overthinking and needed to be approached more mindfully.

2. **Understand Overthinking:** I started questioning the root causes of my anxiety-driven overthinking. Why was I fixating on certain thoughts? What were the fears underlying this cycle? This self-reflection became crucial in understanding and managing my mental state.

3. **Join Social Groups:** Although initially uncomfortable, I learned the value of being part of social groups. Connecting with the Yahoo group and considering the "Art of Living" course reminded me that reaching out to others, even when it felt awkward, could provide valuable support and fresh perspectives.

Through these experiences, I came to realize that chronic anxiety isn't just about the overwhelming emotions in the moment; it has a long-term impact on every facet of life, from personal relationships to career growth.

Overcoming it required not only medication but also lifestyle changes and the creation of support systems that could help break the cycle of negativity and self-doubt.

When Amit left his job and moved on, I found myself once again turning to my alumni network, hoping for guidance and new opportunities. The response was swift and promising.

One of my seniors, now heading a US recruiting and staffing company, offered me a night shift position. The job promised a better salary than my current role, and in my desperation to create a more stable future before approaching Pragati's parents, I eagerly accepted.

Confident in my abilities as a head-hunter, I believed I could thrive in this new role.

Struggling to Keep Up with The World of Recruitment

But the reality of the job soon began to unfold in unexpected ways. The company was a large operation, serving US clients with a team of over 50 recruiters and sales professionals. The environment was fiercely competitive, fast-paced, and driven by high performance.

My boss, one of the top performers, was a constant source of inspiration—an epitome of success and expertise in every aspect of recruitment.

Despite my previous successes, I quickly realized that headhunting was only a small part of what was required for this position. The role demanded proficiency in technical evaluations, screening, and behavioral assessments—tasks that were all carried out over calls. I was completely new to this level of technical scrutiny and lacked the experience to navigate it with confidence.

My seniors, including my boss and another college senior, seemed to perform effortlessly. They could look at a resume and, within seconds, identify a candidate's specialty. Their efficiency was both impressive and intimidating.

The company's cutthroat nature meant that non-performers were regularly let go, heightening my anxiety and making me feel increasingly out of my depth.

As the weeks went by, the pressure intensified. By the third month, performance expectations were overwhelming. Though I managed to secure two selections, it felt more like luck than a true reflection of my abilities.

While my bosses were pleased, I couldn't shake the fear that I wasn't good enough. I spent countless hours overthinking my position, convinced I was on the verge of being fired. The constant stress and fear became a never-ending undercurrent in my life.

The night shift only deepened my sense of isolation, leaving little room for social interaction.

My colleagues noticed my distress and tried to offer support, but I couldn't find the words to explain what I was going through.

The anxiety was all-encompassing, seeping into every aspect of my life.

What should have been routine performance discussions with my bosses turned into negative self-talk, and I questioned everything about myself, my worth, my abilities, and whether I was truly capable.

Meanwhile, my personal life also took a hit.

Pragati had informed her parents about our relationship, and their reaction was explosive. They were furious. First, because their daughter had entered into a love affair, and second, because I had no stability, having just started my career.

The only glimmer of hope was that we shared the same community, Kayastha, which kept a small sliver of hope alive in our calculations.

This period was a harsh reminder of how chronic anxiety can infiltrate every part of your life. The constant pressure, coupled with the ever-present fear of failure, left me in a perpetual state of stress. Feelings of unworthiness and isolation deepened, amplifying the invisible wounds that chronic anxiety leaves in its wake.

Despite external accomplishments, the internal battle with self-doubt and fear was relentless, impacting my performance at work and my personal relationships.

In the midst of this turmoil, one of my batchmates, Gaurav moved in with me. He was a banker with a day job, so our paths mostly crossed on weekends. Though our interactions were limited, his presence was a comforting support someone who had known me deeply since college.

On weekends, we would hang out together, occasionally joined by Abhishek, another close friend. Yet, even in these moments of camaraderie, I remained distant and withdrawn, unable to fully connect as I fought an internal battle, I found it hard to express.

My chronic anxiety never let up, and the anti-depressants I was taking seemed to have little effect. The fear and tension were hard to hide, slipping into my conduct and affecting team meetings.

Perhaps the most challenging aspect was my inability to form new connections at work, the anxiety kept me isolated, making it nearly impossible to bridge the gap between myself and potential friends.

Marriage: Love, Support, and New Beginnings

Meanwhile, Pragati's parents remained steadfastly opposed to our relationship, while my parents, after some persuasion, gradually came around and became supportive. The fact that our sisters were batchmates created a fragile link between our families—a small thread of hope in an otherwise tense situation. Yet, the weight of whether I could truly provide Pragati with the life she deserved hung heavily on me.

Conversations about the cost of living ascended into doubts about my ability to sustain a marriage, further deepening my anxiety.

At work, the tension reached its breaking point when I was summoned for a one-on-one meeting with the Head of Operations. My heart sank, convinced this was the moment I'd been dreading the end of my career.

The night before the meeting, my mind raced with worst-case scenarios, mentally preparing myself for what I thought would be an inevitable dismissal.

To my surprise, the meeting took a different turn. The Head of Operations acknowledged my efforts, pointing out that although my hiring numbers were lower than expected, I was still meeting my quotas and had significant potential.

He presented reports showing that I was spending 70% of my work hours engaging with candidates, far more than my peers. This recognition was a revelation.

Despite my struggles with screening and negotiations, he reassured me that these skills would improve with experience. He encouraged me to continue working hard and even rewarded me with dinner coupons for a luxurious meal at Noida's "The Kebab Factory."

That moment was a breakthrough. Despite the cloud of chronic anxiety, fear, and self-doubt, my hard work was being seen and valued. The acknowledgment from my superior wasn't just about the numbers; it was validation of my perseverance amidst the storm of anxiety.

It was a glimmer of hope that even in the depths of my internal battles, I could still achieve and be recognized.

As time went on, this experience became a defining moment in my journey, propelling me toward success as a renowned head-hunter. It taught me that while chronic anxiety can be debilitating, it is possible to navigate through it.

With the right support, perseverance, and small wins, I realized I could do more than just survive. I could thrive. I allowed myself to take a break, embrace lighter moments, and reconnect with life beyond work. I joined social groups, engaged in conversations, and found joy in simple experiences.

Slowly, my fears became less of a burden and more of a challenge to overcome. Stepping stones toward a future I was beginning to rebuild with confidence.

Temporarily uplifted by the recognition from the company, I continued working. But just as quickly as the cheer appeared, it faded. My mind had become so accustomed to functioning in a perpetual state of crisis that even positive feedback couldn't provide lasting relief.

The shadow of anxiety loomed over every corner of my life, a constant companion.

One of the biggest manifestations of this was my compulsive eating. My anxiety found its expression in food, and I would constantly seek out different places, spending nearly half my income eating out. It wasn't just about the food—it was a frantic attempt to fill an emotional void, to calm the restlessness inside.

One day, a colleague from the sales team mentioned a meditation course by the Art of Living. Desperate for any form of relief, I decided to give it a try. She suggested that, even if it didn't help with my anxiety, at least it would break the monotony and introduce me to new people.

The seven-day course, with its evening sessions and full weekends, became a turning point. It wasn't just about learning meditation techniques like Sudarshan Kriya; it was about meeting seasoned professionals who had mastered their own struggles.

During the course, I connected with a woman who, despite battling severe anxiety, seemed to manage it well alongside her medication. She referred me to her doctor, offering a glimmer of hope.

As if the universe had conspired to align, just as I completed the course, I received an email from Pragati. Her parents had conditionally agreed to our marriage. The timing felt surreal, almost like a divine intervention. I shared the news with my meditation teacher, who smiled and agreed that it was indeed a miracle.

The condition was that the wedding would have to happen within 2-3 months. The pace of events left me dazed, but there was no time to pause and process it all.

I rushed to Gwalior for the family meeting, where, without much ceremony, the engagement was finalized. The whirlwind of events left me stunned. I had hoped for more time. Time to improve my salary, time to mentally prepare. Returning to Noida, I buried myself in work once again.

During this period, Sri Sri Ravi Shankar visited Noida, and I had the chance to meet him. I shared my struggles with anxiety and my uncertainty about the future. He encouraged me to continue with my meditation practice, assuring me that everything would work out in the end.

In spite of these reassurances, my anxiety didn't dissipate. It simply shifted focus—from my job to the impending marriage. The weight of financial insecurity, combined with the fear of the unknown, brewed a relentless cocktail of worry.

My father had been out of work for over a year, adding another layer of financial strain. Thoughts of how we would make ends meet consumed my mind. Even moments of normalcy felt fleeting, as the ever-present anxiety would tighten its grip once more.

Throughout this chaos, Pragati became my source of solace. Our phone conversations offered a brief escape from the mental turmoil I was constantly battling.

As the wedding day drew nearer, I took a leave of absence without pay, knowing it would only add to the financial burden. The preparations, funded largely by my father's diminishing savings, became another overwhelming source of stress. The weight of responsibility and the fear of failure gnawed at me, leading to moments of panic.

Even during the wedding, my anxiety was impossible to mask. The engagement ceremony was a clear signal of my seriousness to everyone, including Pragati. Yet, during the *baraat* (wedding procession) I was consumed by palpitations and an overwhelming urge for the entire event to end.

My friend Gaurav, noticing my distress, offered me a few drinks to calm my nerves, which I gratefully accepted. The wedding ceremony eventually concluded, but my inner turmoil persisted.

After the wedding, we stayed in Gwalior, where I invented a work-related excuse to avoid a honeymoon;

though the true reason was my heightened anxiety. Pragati, ever perceptive, sensed my unease but chose not to push the issue.

Her silent understanding offered a small comfort amidst the chaos brewing inside me.

This period of my life was a stark reminder of how chronic anxiety can seep into every facet of existence. From professional accomplishments to personal milestones, fear, self-doubt, and anticipatory dread never loosened their grip.

Even moments that should have been joyous were tainted by anxiety, turning celebrations into burdens to endure.

Returning to work after the wedding, I briefly felt a sense of relief from my internal struggles. A celebratory office party with friends offered a temporary distraction, but soon, the familiar pressures of work and persistent anxiety came rushing back. The mounting workload, combined with my internal fears, overwhelmed me.

Even minor issues at work triggered disproportionate reactions, making me feel as though my entire world was collapsing. Despite knowing that these fears were often irrational, I felt powerless to control them.

To cope, I established a personal rule: whenever anxiety flared up, I would step away from my desk, taking a walk or having a smoke to collect my thoughts. Solitude became my refuge during these moments.

I also turned to motivational books, hoping for solace and guidance. Books like *I Can Win* and Dale Carnegie's classics offered valuable insights, but they didn't alleviate my deep-seated anxiety.

What I truly needed was a mentor or coach to help channel my thoughts and energy in a more constructive way. Unfortunately, such guidance wasn't available in the high-pressure, competitive environment I worked in.

While my seniors and bosses were supportive, the fast-paced nature of the job left little room for personal mentorship.

In the meantime, I had moved to Noida alone, as Pragati was finishing her final semester. We had planned for her to join me after six months, but after just three months, the night shifts started taking a serious toll on my health.

Sleepless nights and constant restlessness, fuelled by anxiety, made it increasingly hard to function.

When I confided in a friend, he suggested switching to a day job for more stability. Hoping for some direction, I reached out to my alumni network, but the response was tepid. Many people advised me to avoid job-hopping and to focus on settling into a stable role instead.

Four months after her exams, Pragati finally moved in with me. Balancing the demands of my night shifts and our new life together proved to be a challenge. Despite my efforts to maintain a sense of normalcy, my anxiety simmered just beneath the surface.

Pragati, with her own aspirations, and I spent time visiting malls and dining out, but the underlying tension never left. Her parents visited to help us set up our home, but even their presence couldn't dissolve the strain.

I found myself struggling to hide my anxiety, even considering changing doctors in search of better management.

The mounting challenges like my demanding job, our marriage, and financial pressures created a constant storm of fear and uncertainty. While my salary was decent, the persistent negativity I felt seemed inescapable.

The only refuge I found was in my work, where my meticulous efforts allowed me to meet targets and maintain a hint of professional success.

But the stress began to seep into our personal lives. Tensions led to outbursts at home, resulting in occasional arguments with Pragati. Our parents stepped in to mediate, but Pragati's parents grew increasingly concerned about my mental state.

I tried to explain my anxiety, but it was a concept they struggled to understand. In an effort to grasp my condition better, they even met with my doctor. In the middle of all this, I took on tutoring gig, hoping they would provide some semblance of stability in my life.

A New Opportunity, But the Internal Struggle Continues

Just when the chaos felt overwhelming, a lifeline appeared. I received a call from an IT multinational establishing a Hiring Research Cell in India. My previous headhunting experience proved invaluable, and I was offered a contract position. The compensation was attractive, and crucially, it was a day job. Exactly what I needed.

The role was part of a pilot project, and while its long-term future was uncertain, I decided to seize the opportunity. The expats who interviewed me were impressed with my skills, and I saw this as a chance to escape the limitations of my previous role and finally strive for a more balanced life.

This job was everything I'd hoped for and more. My first assignment was a dream project: hire 100 fresh graduates in just four weeks. A tight deadline, but a challenge I relished.

I devised a clear strategy, leveraging candidate referrals and the offline social networks that were the primary talent source at the time, long before LinkedIn and Orkut.

By effectively tapping into these channels, I single-handedly completed the assignment ahead of schedule. The results were impressive, earning me high praise from colleagues and superiors.

I rejoiced in the satisfaction of successfully tackling this high-volume hiring task. Soon after, I was tasked with establishing the Hiring Research Cell. My first step was a meticulous mapping of companies by skill set and domain—a crucial foundation for identifying and sourcing talent.

With this groundwork laid, I began mapping candidates to those specific skill sets. The process proved remarkably effective, and I consistently exceeded expectations, earning recognition for my dedication and results.

However, beneath this veneer of professional success, a significant problem was brewing. Despite excelling at my work, I struggled to integrate into the company culture. The office environment was vibrant, energetic, and characterized by a camaraderie that I found difficult to navigate.

My colleagues were outgoing, often socializing through parties and group activities, but I remained cautious, unsure how to participate without feeling exposed and out of place. I couldn't quite manage to "act normal," as one colleague later put it.

I was often perceived as too serious, not laughing enough, and a bit too "rough around the edges" compared to the company's relaxed atmosphere. I felt like a perpetual outsider, watching the fun from a distance, unable to truly join in.

This cultural disconnect exacerbated my existing anxiety, which was already a constant undercurrent in my life. Social interactions became daunting, and I found it difficult to relax in such a high-energy environment.

I tried to force myself to participate, to become part of the team, but the anxiety made me hyper-vigilant and self-conscious. Having no prior experience in such a dynamic, social workplace, my anxiety transformed simply "fitting in" into a constant uphill battle.

Current Career: Purpose, Passion, and Impact

Home offered little respite. My anxiety manifested as constant restlessness, making even simple daily tasks feel overwhelming. My thoughts raced, a relentless whirlwind that never allowed me a moment of peace.

Even basic conversations or transactions felt like monumental hurdles, often forcing me to step away from my desk just to catch my breath.

These brief breaks during the workday became my lifeline. Short respites from the overwhelming tide of anxiety that seemed to follow me everywhere.

As a coping mechanism, I threw myself into my work, pushing myself to work longer and longer hours. Since candidates were primarily available after 5 PM, I began working intensely from 5 to 8 PM, often making 50 to 100 calls during that window. This extra effort kept my mind occupied, a distraction from the constant, underlying restlessness.

My focus on work, my commitment to delivering results, became my escape from the anxiety that permeated every facet of my life.

I quickly became known in the recruitment industry for my headhunting prowess.

Technical professionals across various sectors knew me, and I began receiving inbound leads from candidates seeking new opportunities.

I maintained a meticulously organized data system, staying on top of my game and constantly refining my approach. Despite my internal struggles, I managed to perform at a high level.

However, I knew that my success was built on sheer effort and discipline, rather than any sense of ease or genuine enjoyment.

Eventually, my contract was extended, but with it came feedback: I needed to adjust to the company culture.

My professional achievements were praised, but it was clear that my approach of working tirelessly without engaging socially or participating in the fun was unsustainable, both for me and for the company.

The feedback felt like a wake-up call, highlighting a deeper issue.

My ability to succeed in the role was being undermined by my inability to truly integrate into the team. The relentless drive to perform, coupled with my internal anxiety, had left me isolated and disconnected from the very culture I had hoped to be a part of.

This feedback became a turning point. I realized that no matter how successful I was professionally, the lack of balance between work and personal connection was taking a severe toll on my well-being.

It became clear that true success wasn't just about hitting targets and completing assignments. It was about finding a way to navigate both professional and personal challenges in a way that fostered balance, integration, and, most importantly, mental peace.

As our hiring volume increased, the need for more effective candidate filtering, especially on the technical side, became apparent. To address this, a training program was implemented, covering essential concepts like the software development life cycle, technical terminology, and design and architecture principles.

This initiative opened up a whole new world for me. I embraced the opportunity wholeheartedly, immersing myself in these concepts. I began shadowing technical interviews, expanding my technical knowledge, and devouring any relevant material I could find.

Armed with a deeper understanding of the technical aspects and my existing talent-mapping skills, my candidate selection rate improved dramatically.

I consistently surpassed my hiring targets, gaining confidence in my ability to effectively blend technical knowledge with recruitment expertise.

Our team expanded during this period, and I had the opportunity to hire a fresh graduate. Anuj, who had a BBA from Jumba followed by an MCA, was eager to transition into recruitment. Initially, I dismissed his determination, but after several conversations, I agreed to an interview. With some persuasion, he was hired.

Anuj went on to stay with the company for over eight years and even followed our manager to three subsequent organizations. His dedication and growth were a testament to the talent development opportunities we fostered, both for our clients and within our own team.

During one of my headhunting campaigns, I came across a technically exceptional candidate who wasn't interested in the opportunity we offered.

Despite my best efforts, he remained loyal to his current, little-known company.

Intrigued by his pride and confidence in his organization, I decided to learn more.

The Luckiest Cold Call

As I started cold calling leads, it became clear that this company was no ordinary player. A small firm, it had attracted top talent from prestigious institutions like IITs and NITs. The candidates I spoke to were confident and deeply proud of the company's values and vision, sparking my curiosity even further.

In my talent mapping process, I connected with a senior leader at the company. After hearing my pitch, he politely declined, and later, I spoke to the HR head, who also firmly rejected my headhunting efforts, assuring me no one would leave.

Yet, he invited me for coffee that evening. I was taken aback but accepted, eager to learn more.

Over coffee, the HR head shared the company's vision: currently a team of under 200 employees, they planned to grow to 5,000 within five years. His enthusiasm was contagious, and I was soon introduced to the Co-Founder, Rajul, whose energy mirrored the HR head's. By the end of the meeting, I had an offer in hand— the tables had turned.

What gave them such confidence? Their team of 200 brilliant minds from top-tier colleges seemed to be on the right track. With high compensation and a compelling vision, the opportunity was too good to ignore.

Despite the attraction, I reached out to JUMBA alumni and friends for advice. Everyone warned that leaving an MNC for a start-up was risky. So, I held back accepting the offer, explaining to the human resources head, Umesh, that I needed more time. He made one last attempt to convince me, but I stood firm. We agreed to reconnect in six months.

Looking back, this experience taught me valuable lessons in risk management and trust in my instincts. What started as a cold call evolved into a career-altering opportunity, deepening my appreciation for the unpredictable nature of career choices and the hidden potential in unexpected places.

I stayed in my headhunting role, but despite success, I grew increasingly dissatisfied. The job felt disconnected from the more dynamic, client-facing aspects of recruitment. Though my work in sourcing candidates was effective, I craved more direct interaction with clients and candidates.

More troubling was the growing unease at the company. In spite of my performance, I struggled to fit into the culture, which fuelled anxiety and restlessness. Medication and meditation didn't provide lasting relief, and the discomfort started affecting my personal life. I buried myself in work to cope, but the anxiety remained. My manager,

Ashu noticed and offered support, but I couldn't break free from the cycle.

In desperation, I consulted an astrologer, hoping for answers, but nothing seemed to ease the constant pressure I felt. Simple activities, like going out with my wife, Pragati, became overwhelming, and panic attacks left me drained.

A few colleagues noticed my struggles, offering concern and support, but the tension lingered. Then, Umesh, the Human Resources Manager I had been working with, shared that his company was expanding and moving to Noida.

The excitement of the growing company sparked a spark of hope.

After months of uncertainty, I decided to accept the offer. The opportunity for full-cycle recruiting in a dynamic company felt like a fresh start. When I resigned, Ashu was reluctant to let me go, offering to adjust my role, but I felt it was time to move on. Before I left, he reassured me that my skills were valuable and that I would excel in my career, which boosted my confidence.

Looking back, I realize that the discomfort I felt was a catalyst for change. It pushed me to seek something better—an opportunity that allowed me to thrive. Leaving that familiar environment opened up new possibilities I hadn't imagined.

I threw myself into my role, constantly learning and applying new ideas. One of my most exciting projects was hiring for leadership positions, and I humorously called myself "Hiring Express" for the speed and intensity of the work.

The company was growing fast, and recruiting became a critical, revenue-generating function. Despite the immense pressure, we had a lot of power and responsibility, with high stakes at play.

Hiring was no easy task. Internal interviews were tough, and client interviews were even more challenging. Given the company's size, convincing candidates to join after an offer was an art in itself. I used my international experience to tap into talent from the US and Europe, filling critical roles with talent from top companies like Microsoft and Yahoo.

We celebrated our wins with weekend events and parties, thriving in a vibrant, energetic environment. My manager, Umesh, was empowering—covering for my mistakes and letting me learn from them.

Then, campus hiring became a dream come true. I visited top engineering institutes like the IITs, and later expanded to Gwalior Colleges to give back to my alma mater.

My travels across India enriched both my personal and professional life.

Working on leadership hiring gave me the chance to converse with senior VPs, Sandeep and Manish, whose insights on business and growth significantly expanded my understanding.

While still junior, my work ethic helped me form strong, lifelong friendships with these leaders.

However, despite my professional success, anxiety still plagued me. Panic attacks, though less frequent, continued to affect my personal life. Late nights at work and social events took priority over family time, and meditation alone couldn't ease the feelings of worthlessness.

After switching doctors, the medication adjustments caused side effects like weight gain, adding to my struggles.

A major emotional setback came when my father lost his employment case in the High Court. It deeply affected me, and my anxiety worsened. Despite introspection, I couldn't pinpoint the cause of my turmoil, leaving me feeling like I was fighting an internal battle I couldn't win.

As the company grew, I gained recognition, especially in leadership hiring. I expanded my network and honed my skills, working with co-founders in the US.

At the same time, my wife and I were expecting our first child, adding both excitement and new responsibilities to my life.

The challenges I faced during this period, both professionally and personally taught me invaluable lessons about resilience.

The pressure of leadership hiring, working with senior leaders, and personal struggles all intertwined, shaping my ability to handle life's ups and downs. It wasn't just about recruiting; it was about managing anxiety, learning from mistakes, and staying focused on the end goal.

The company's explosive growth brought immense pressure. As we expanded, tensions arose between old and new practices, and the cultural fabric shifted.

The influx of new employees made it harder to maintain the company's original spirit, while the pressure to meet numbers was intense. Despite the challenges, my passion for the company kept me grounded.

In the middle of this, the rise of social media, especially LinkedIn, transformed recruiting. Initially doubtful, I soon welcomed it, realizing its power to connect talent and opportunities globally. This digital shift reshaped the recruiting landscape, and those who couldn't adapt were left behind.

During this time, my father faced a major setback, losing a high-profile case and suffering a cardiac arrest. While he physically recovered, the emotional toll of job loss deeply affected our family.

My sister, fresh out of college, joined an IT services company in HR, adding more change to my life. The pressure and uncertainty intensified, leaving me more anxious than ever.

Sales Growth Through Anxiety

Despite this, I had learned to manage my anxiety. The company I worked for was rapidly expanding, acquiring firms in Eastern Europe and India. Amid this growth, a new sales head, Chetan, was appointed, setting my life on a new course.

He introduced me to a project to acquire smaller product companies, and soon, he invited me to join the sales team.

Though anxious about the leap, Chetan reassured me with his mentorship, and I decided to take the risk. At the same time, a former colleague, Sandeep, offered me a role in his new venture, adding to my confusion. After discussions with Manish, Sandeep, and Pragati, I decided to stay with Chetan, seeing it as an opportunity for growth and mentorship.

As I transitioned, my anxiety flared, especially during client meetings. Despite the discomfort, I pushed through.

One lead I shared with Chetan eventually became one of our largest clients in India, proving that anxiety, though limiting, can drive growth. Facing this challenge helped me embrace change rather than resist it.

For anyone struggling with similar anxieties, remember anxiety signals growth. Lean into the discomfort, and it can transform you.

I transitioned to the India Sales team with a mix of excitement and doubt. While leadership was skeptical about the Indian market, especially with pricing concerns, Chetan, our sales head, mentored me through the process.

Despite the challenges, I began generating leads, and success came quickly. Corporate India was responding. However, anxiety still lingered, especially during face-to-face meetings, where my nervousness was noticeable.

After a difficult meeting, Chetan noticed my tense demeanor and offered a piece of advice that stuck with me: "Even if you're afraid inside, act strong on the outside."

His words weren't just about masking anxiety they were about building confidence and learning to manage pressure in high-stakes situations.

Having the right support and guidance in moments of self-doubt can make all the difference.

Chetan's mentorship gave me the reassurance and perspective I needed to push forward, proving that sometimes, external encouragement can help us unlock strengths we don't yet see in ourselves.

Things Anxiety Makes You Do at Work

Work anxiety is like an overzealous intern in your brain. It constantly interrupts, overanalyses, and assumes the worst.

While everyone experiences work stress, anxiety takes it to another level, turning routine tasks into mini emotional rollercoasters.

If you've ever found yourself in these situations, welcome to the club.

1. The Email Spiral of Doom

You write a simple email:

"Hey, just checking on the sales report. Let me know its status. Thanks!"

Then anxiety kicks in. *Does "let me know" sound too demanding?*

Should I add a smiley face to soften it? No, that's unprofessional. Maybe just 'Thanks!'—but what if that sounds cold?

Result?

You rewrite the email 10 times, overthink every word, and finally send it—only to immediately reread it in your Sent folder, convinced you made a mistake.

2. The "Can We Talk?" Heart Attack

Your boss messages you: "Hey, can we talk?"

Logical brain: *Maybe it's just a routine check-in.*

Anxious brain: *I'm getting fired. My career is over. What will I tell my family?*

You spend the next 10 minutes spiraling, mentally updating your resume, calculating how long you can survive without a job, and regretting that one email you sent three months ago.

The actual conversation? *"Just wanted to say great job on that project!"*

3. The Instant Regret of Speaking Up in a Meeting

You finally muster the courage to share an idea. People nod. The discussion moves on.

But instead of feeling accomplished, your anxiety whispers: *Wait, was that dumb? Did I talk too much? Did I interrupt someone? Should I clarify?*

For the next hour, you replay the moment in your head while pretending to listen.

It's All in Your Head (Literally)

Anxiety at work is exhausting, but the good news is - you're not alone.

Most of the things we stress about never actually happen, and the rest?

No one is paying nearly as much attention as we think they are.

Sales Expansion and Personal Growth

Soon after, Chetan arranged for me to travel to the US for training at our headquarters, marking a significant milestone in my career.

While there, I immersed myself in reading The Last Mughal by William Dalrymple. Reading it deepened my understanding of history beyond the textbook version I had grown up with. It sparked an intellectual curiosity about power, politics, and historical narratives, compelling me to explore further.

Soon, I found myself delving into political ideologies, historical events, and global revolutions, drawing parallels between the past and present.

My manager, Manoj, offered me a full-time position in the USA. Overjoyed, I immediately accepted. My supportive colleague, Chetan, offered his sincere congratulations.

Arriving in the US in February 2007, just as my daughter turned one, was a new chapter. I admired everything—the wide roads, the cleanliness, the food. The work was challenging but exciting, with a focus on lead generation for the Captive Acquisition project.

Cold calling and research took center stage, but I persevered, overcoming initial resistance and handling objections with growing confidence. This experience, and my ability to manage anxiety, marked a significant personal and professional growth.

My role expanded into sales operations, encompassing tasks like organizing meetings, win-loss analysis, SugarCRM management, and paperwork. It was a smaller scale, but a new challenge. I'd never worked in this capacity before, and the learning curve was steep.

We agreed on a three-month US integration period before my visa was finalized, after which I'd return to India to bring over my family. Compensation was negotiated, and everything seemed to be falling into place.

But even with this career advancement, my anxiety resurfaced. Palpitations and uncertainty crept in. Was this move the right decision? The US cost of living was daunting. How secure was the Captive project? The familiar fear returned. Despite the excitement, worries began to fester.

A significant challenge emerged: our target market wasn't as robust as we'd initially thought. Some captives operated at unexpectedly low costs, and many target companies were service-based, not product-based. Despite this, I refined the list and generated a few leads, but most stalled in the sales pipeline.

On the sales operations side, mastering SugarCRM was a hurdle. Creating reports, tracking pipelines, and following up was demanding. But with support from the CEO, co-founder, and senior team members, I learned quickly. The close-knit office environment fostered learning and growth.

The Self-Made Dilemma

While Pragati and my parents were excited about our move to the USA, I struggled with self-doubt and anxiety.

Despite the incredible opportunity, I couldn't shake the worry:

- *Was it the right move?*
- *Would I meet expectations?*

I also felt overwhelmed by this opportunity.

One major source of anxiety was realizing that the captive opportunity wasn't as large as we'd hoped. With more free time, I grew concerned about the future. I shared these doubts with Manoj, my supportive boss, who reassured me.

He acknowledged the smaller prospect list but reminded me of the growing importance of my role in sales and recruiting, even hinting at an incentive plan.

Back at work, I felt the weight of my mental struggle. My mind seemed focused on the negative, fuelling my stress. Reading complex texts was my escape, but it only intensified my anxiety.

Despite this, I threw myself into work, making countless calls and facing a slow response. But after weeks of persistence, I managed to secure some engagement and learned valuable lessons.

At our annual sales conference in Virginia, I found an opportunity with a telecom account, which also opened doors for onsite recruiting. With Manoj's approval, we had great success filling onsite roles, proving the potential of this model. I used this success to encourage others and expand our approach.

Meanwhile, on the captive side, leads were still slow, but after persistent effort, I managed to secure two promising opportunities.

Unfortunately, they didn't close, but the experience taught me valuable lessons about business development, client negotiations, and the challenges of converting leads into tangible results.

After a year, we decided to focus on inbound leads for captives rather than actively pursuing new ones.

Though we didn't close any captive deals, the progress in onsite recruiting and sales operations gave us hope for the year ahead.

The Weight of Anxiety

But amidst the professional excitement, anxiety took a more intense hold. I became consumed with thoughts of stability like financial security, long-term prospects, and an uncertain future.

It wasn't just career growth anymore; it was about whether I could make this move work and if the dream of a better life would slip away.

I turned to my doctor for help and was prescribed a mood stabilizer, but the anxiety persisted. Despite a good job, a decent life, and even a friend of Pragati's moving into our community, my mind couldn't escape the constant *"what ifs."*

I confided in trusted colleagues, Chetan and Manish, who reassured me that this experience would be invaluable for my growth.

But the pressure continued to build, and the weight felt personal, not just a result of the market instability.

As my anxiety grew, it strained my relationships. Pragati bore the brunt of my irritability, and I became consumed by my worries, even losing joy in the small things.

At the same time, I found an unexpected escape in discussions with a young colleague, Sarath, whose passion for Marxist ideas drew me into new intellectual realms. But this only deepened my internal tension, leading me to question everything about myself and my life.

Navigating the Crisis

The 2008 financial crisis sent shockwaves through the global economy, leaving businesses scrambling to stay afloat. Layoffs, hiring freezes, and uncertainty dominated the corporate world, and while I managed to keep my role intact, the stress of navigating this turbulent period took a toll on my health.

A cataract developed at a young age, a stark reminder that the relentless stress and negative thinking were not just mental burdens but were manifesting physically.

Despite the instability in the market, I continued to hit my recruiting targets, and the company's revenue showed steady growth. On the surface, I was succeeding.

Yet internally, anxiety never loosened its grip. As companies downsized and financial fears loomed, my inner demons seemed impossible to escape.

By 2009, the company underwent a major restructuring, bringing in a new president with a fresh perspective. There was uncertainty, but also new opportunities.

A major deal demanded a rapid influx of talent in the Bay Area, creating the perfect storm. I was asked to fly to California and spearhead the hiring initiative, tasked with recruiting 30 to 50 people in just a few weeks.

It felt like a breakthrough moment. I thrived under pressure, successfully hiring thirty people in four weeks, earning the nickname "The Hiring Express." It was a professional high, proof that I could deliver even in the toughest of times.

But anxiety doesn't care about success. No matter how well things were going, the palpitations, negative thoughts, and underlying fear of failure never left. The external crisis had passed for many, but inside me, the battle raged on.

As my career progressed, so did my intellectual curiosity. I delved deep into political ideologies, comparative religion, and philosophy, exploring different perspectives that both fascinated and consumed me. What started as a passion for knowledge soon became an obsession, and before I realized it, I was isolating myself, questioning everything, detaching from the familiar, and feeling disconnected from the life I once knew.

Meanwhile, the company was growing rapidly, and with that growth came increased expectations and structural changes. Then came an abrupt reality check that it was time to move back to India.

Unlike an exciting new career shift, this decision wasn't mine to make. It was forced upon me due to circumstances beyond my control.

I explored every possible option to stay in the U.S. and secured two job offers—one from a competitor and another from a vendor. Both companies sponsored my H1 visa applications, giving me hope that my experience and track record would secure my place.

However, both visa applications were rejected, closing off my last chance to continue my career in the U.S. My options were now severely limited, and reality sank in, I had no choice but to return to India. It wasn't a smooth transition, nor was it a decision I embraced. Instead, it felt like I was being forced out of a life I had worked tirelessly to build.

As the pressure mounted, I sought ways to manage my stress. I enrolled in an Art of Living retreat, hoping to find peace amid the chaos. The experience brought temporary relief, but the sense of unease never truly left.

My neck pain persisted, an undeniable physical manifestation of my internal turmoil. The tension I felt wasn't just mental; my body was carrying the weight of my anxiety.

It was no longer a matter of choice or hope; my time in the U.S. had come to an end. Returning to India after three years wasn't a fresh start, it felt like a setback, a loss of everything I had built.

Returning to India was bittersweet. While I felt a sense of loss leaving behind my life in the U.S., I was also excited about contributing in a meaningful way. The company had grown significantly over the past three years, headcount had nearly quadrupled, and operations had expanded into Eastern Europe. I was given the option to join either Sales or Talent Acquisition in Noida or Bangalore.

I chose Noida, as it was the company's headquarters, and opted for Talent Acquisition, my area of expertise. My U.S. exposure had strengthened my skills, but deep down, I feared handling sales due to my anxiety.

However, there was skepticism about my ability to lead. Critics pointed out that I had never managed a team and had always operated as an individual contributor, they doubted whether I could handle the scale of the role in India. They weren't entirely wrong.

To make matters more challenging, internal competition in the recruiting team was fierce, and some of my peers saw me as a threat. Despite these doubts, I was assigned to the Telecom Business Unit, a troubled and notoriously difficult division. Though I had built strong relationships with key stakeholders in the U.S., there were serious concerns about whether I could deliver results in this tough environment, even I had my doubts.

One of my first challenges was rescuing a struggling team member. A senior recruiter, Rashmi was on the verge of termination, placed on a performance improvement plan by his manager.

I had known him from my early career, a seasoned professional who understood the company well. Despite his struggles, I believed he had potential. Instead of letting him go, I requested HR to extend his exit and brought him onto my team.

Fortunately, I had one strong advantage. The new Global Talent Head was someone I had personally hired. This created an immediate connection, giving me the opportunity to prove myself in this new chapter of my career.

As a year passed, the new Talent Head introduced sweeping changes, triggering resistance and high attrition. Many long-time employees left, and while I had my own differences, I saw no immediate reason to move. However, I began to realize that advancing to a senior role required stronger soft skills, an area where I needed mentorship and guidance.

After seven years with the company, I lacked direct mentoring, which made professional growth challenging.

During this challenging period, the company was undergoing a significant slowdown, restructuring its client base and delivery model. This forced many long-time employees, including myself, to adapt to the new changes, increasing the pressure on everyone.

As the workload and expectations grew, my anxieties resurfaced, particularly during difficult discussions with my team. However, as I navigated through this, I discovered something important: I wasn't alone in my struggles.

I learned that two of my senior colleagues, Latish and Ajay, were also grappling with their own anxiety. Although both of them initially tried to conceal their struggles, eventually they opened up to me, and we formed a support system for one another.

It was a relief to realize that anxiety wasn't something I was facing in isolation. It was affecting others at a senior level as well.

Together, we shared our experiences and ways of coping. Latish and Ajay suggested I explore alternative methods to manage my inner turmoil, and that's when I tried acupressure and reiki.

It was a turning point for me, as these practices helped me find some relief from the stress, and more importantly, it gave me a deeper sense of connection with my colleagues.

We weren't just colleagues anymore; we had become a support system for each other, sharing both the burdens and the solutions to manage our anxiety.

Rumors of job cuts in the Talent team added to my stress. Despite my track record and recognition, I immediately assumed the worst that I would be the first to go.

My self-doubt overshadowed reality, making it difficult to function.

Even though the new HR Head appreciated my work, my inability to acknowledge my own contributions left me feeling vulnerable.

A Journey Through Self-Doubt and Change

In my panic, I reached out to my network for opportunities. Ashu, now at a Big 5 firm, connected me with leading companies in India, and soon, I started receiving calls.

When the promotion cycle came around, my promotion to Senior Manager was deferred. That was a huge blow to my morale. Feeling unappreciated and restless, I intensified my job search, determined to move forward.

I secured two job offers. One from Ashu's company and another from a leading IT firm. With that, I made the decision to resign.

But instead of relief, anxiety hit me harder than ever. My palpitations intensified, and suddenly, I wasn't afraid of starting a new job. I was terrified of leaving my current one. The uncertainty gnawed at me, and as the stress mounted, my neck pain resurfaced, serving as a harsh reminder of how deeply anxiety affected me.

The thought of joining a new company sent me into a spiral of panic. I worried about my anxiety, my ability to handle pressure, and whether I would succeed in a new environment. Ashu had high expectations, but he reassured me that I would do well.

Seeking more advice, I spoke to senior colleagues Latish, Ajay, and a senior finance executive. They all encouraged me to take the leap, reminding me that I was getting a significant salary hike and a major designation upgrade.

Still, I was paralyzed by self-doubt. My current company accepted me as I was, and in some ways, my anxiety had become a strength in that environment. Torn between excitement and fear, I decided to discuss my dilemma with my manager.

In my moment of extreme uncertainty, I reached out to a trusted colleague in the U.S., who immediately recognized my crippling self-doubt. He suggested I attend a meditation retreat called "Alpha Mind Power", which happened to have a session the following week. He insisted I couldn't afford to miss it.

I signed up for the two-day intensive meditation retreat, and what happened next was nothing short of a revelation. My chronic neck pain disappeared completely. The instructor explained that it was emotional stress manifesting physically.

That experience was so profound that I went on to complete eight levels of the course over the next few years.

A Tough Decision Between Two Opportunities

As I prepared for my exit, I was hit with another surprise. The company didn't want me to leave. Senior leadership told me I was performing exceptionally well and had big opportunities ahead.

My boss had resigned, and the new HR Head, Sanjay, was taking on additional responsibilities. After several meetings with the HR Head and Country Manager, they offered me a promotion and the role of India Hiring Head.

The decision became even more complicated. Pragati and I were expecting our second daughter, and I believed she would bring good luck. If I took the job with Ashu, I would have to relocate to Hyderabad, while my other offer was in Bangalore.

Meanwhile, Sanjay had become an incredible mentor, which had been one of the key reasons I was considering leaving in the first place.

More than anything, the thought of leading India Recruiting felt like a deeply personal investment I had seen the company grow, had countless ideas for improvement, and felt emotionally connected to its success.

I was overwhelmed, panicked, and utterly torn. But in the end, I decided to stay. It felt safer to be with a company that knew and valued me.

But staying came at a cost. Ashu took it personally, and it took two to three years to mend our relationship. Looking back, I realize I could have handled the situation better. But at that moment, I had to choose stability over uncertainty—even if the decision wasn't easy.

On October 20, 2011, we welcomed our younger daughter, Mishi, into the world. They say daughters bring luck, and I couldn't agree more—her arrival filled our lives with joy, love, and new beginnings.

A New Role, A New Challenge

Stepping into my new role felt like a dream come true—a validation that my hard work and dedication had finally been recognized.

I've always believed that sincere efforts pay off, sooner or later, and this moment felt like proof of that. Coincidentally, I was the seventh Talent Acquisition Head in seven years, and with seven being my lucky number, it felt like a good omen for what lay ahead.

At the time, work was relatively slow, giving us much-needed breathing room to plan for the road ahead. Rashmi was by my side, performing well, and we began laying the groundwork for future success.

However, working under Sanjay was a completely different experience. He was driven, passionate, and full of ideas, pushing for multiple initiatives and detailed reports with a distinctive leadership style.

It took time to align with his vision, but once we understood his priorities and approach, we quickly found our rhythm. A new era of aggressive growth was about to unfold.

With new responsibilities came a steep learning curve. The pressure was immense, and I knew we had to build a strong foundation to sustain long-term success. I decided to focus on sourcing, implementing specialized training to help the team leverage passive candidates and internal databases more effectively.

To further strengthen our efforts, we hired two interns dedicated exclusively to managing the passive talent pool, while the rest of the team continued enhancing their skills.

One of my key proposals was to provide laptops to all recruiters, allowing for higher productivity and flexible work options. At the time, only managers and above had laptops, so this was a significant shift. Sanjay fully supported the idea, recognizing the need for efficiency and adaptability.

We started seeing positive results, but the demand kept surging, and we needed a game-changer. The company decided to invest in LinkedIn, and Sanjay tasked me with building the business case. Once we secured approval, we went all in, optimizing the platform to elevate our hiring strategy.

However, with rising expectations came overwhelming pressure. Weekend drives, late hours, and constant escalations became the norm. Vendor agencies could only help so much, and the intensity of hiring demands reached a boiling point.

In the face of relentless stress, my anxiety spiraled. Each escalation sent me into a deep cycle of negative thinking, where my instinct was to look for an escape rather than face the chaos head-on.

The constant pressure made relaxation feel impossible. I was always on edge, always anticipating the next crisis. The weight of expectations was crushing, and I struggled to find balance in the storm.

The LinkedIn Case Study That Changed Everything

When we first started using LinkedIn, we weren't getting the results we expected. With only two licenses, we were essentially tapping into the same active job seeker pool available across other platforms. Frustrated, I told Sanjay that it didn't seem as effective as we had hoped.

Sanjay paused and then said something that changed my perspective: "If it's not working for you, then something is wrong with your approach. Maybe you need to take a step back and critically review what you're doing."

He was right. I took a closer look at our strategy, and after a deep dive, we realized that we were using LinkedIn like a traditional job board, which was completely missing the platform's true potential.

Recognizing the need for a fundamental shift, we re-evaluated our approach. Rashmi and the rest of the team joined in on a brainstorming session, identifying key changes we needed to implement. We refined our outreach, optimized engagement tactics, and leveraged passive talent more effectively. Once we made these adjustments, the results improved dramatically.

With my new role also came extensive travel to locations like Bangalore, Nagpur, and various campuses across India. Fortunately, I enjoyed traveling and exploring new places, but much of it was focused on handling escalations and ensuring smooth operations. It was an exhausting but necessary part of the journey.

Once we cracked the right way to use LinkedIn, everything fell into place. We expanded our network, built a proactive talent database, and optimized our hiring strategy. These adjustments led to significant improvements across all key metrics.

As the team grew, we brought in new hires, injecting fresh ideas into our processes. Many of us old-timers, myself included, had been stuck in a fixed mindset, and this new energy revitalized the team.

Among the standout recruits was Rajiv, a phenomenal recruiter with an exceptional ability to close hires.

Sanjay insisted on personally interviewing every new team member, and we had a difference of opinion on hiring Rajiv. However, after much debate, he agreed, and it turned out to be the right decision. Rajiv became a top performer, earning the reputation of a hiring machine.

Our professional connection didn't end there; he later worked with me in two other companies.

Meanwhile, Rashmi received an outstanding offer and decided to move on.

During one of my work trips to Bangalore, I took the opportunity to advance my Alpha Mind Meditation practice. Since the teacher had stopped visiting Delhi, I had to travel to attend sessions, but it was worth every effort.

The experience was deeply transformative.

On the social front, I represented Delhi/NCR at a national executive meeting in Bangalore to review IT Milan's progress. A generational gap was emerging between the new and old formats, creating tensions in execution.

However, the Milans continued to grow, and we were meeting our objectives despite these challenges.

At work, my exposure was expanding beyond recruitment. I started meeting clients alongside delivery leaders, gaining firsthand insight into broader business operations.

Our team consistently met or exceeded targets, reinforcing our growing impact within the company.

The Cost of Success: Anxiety, Overwork, and a Search for Balance

With success came a cost. I had become a workaholic, constantly working late, obsessing over candidate searches, and struggling to switch off. After work, the team and I would often go out for casual get-togethers, returning home even later. Looking back, I realize this wasn't just about work, but it was another escape from my anxiety and depression.

Sanjay noticed my deteriorating work-life balance and advised me to moderate my hours and take breaks. He even visited our home to check in on me. Pragati and my mother also expressed concerns, but I couldn't help it.

I simply didn't enjoy lighter moments. My mind constantly needed a problem to solve and if there wasn't one, it would create one.

It was exhausting and, in hindsight, a complete waste of energy.

My fear of high-pressure situations only fueled my anxiety further, often leading to conflicts with stakeholders. However, Sanjay managed these situations for me, ensuring that despite my struggles, we continued to deliver results.

By now, Sanjay was fully aware of my anxiety issues, and he encouraged me to explore philosophical perspectives. He had a deep interest in psychology and organizational development, and our relationship evolved beyond just mentor-mentee. Though his leadership style was intense, he genuinely wanted to help me grow.

Through my readings, I discovered the works of Acharya Shriram Sharma and Yogananda Paramhansa, both of whom provided deep insights into mental stress and depression.

Their writings emphasized that anxiety stems from overthinking and that a healthy mind requires balance with lighthearted conversations, laughter, and rest.

Without these, the negative loop of emotions and actions becomes a vicious cycle.

To gain deeper self-awareness, Sanjay approved psychometric tests for me. They were eye-opening. I also started Reiki sessions at Arvind Ashram, led by a senior government official and Reiki Grandmaster. I continued these sessions for over three years.

In addition, I tried homeopathic treatments from a well-known doctor in Noida, hoping for some relief.

Despite having everything I had ever wanted like career success, a good role, and a supportive family. I still felt undeserving, on edge, and emotionally drained. It's difficult to explain, but no matter how much I achieved, there was always a lingering emptiness.

Sanjay, recognizing my struggles, encouraged me to attend public speaking sessions to help build confidence. I was excited but nervous.

My first session was with senior professionals from top companies, and though I prepared extensively, I felt an overwhelming sense of self-doubt.

However, over time, I grew comfortable. I even started bringing my team members to these sessions. Eventually, I realized that these events were more about networking than real knowledge-sharing. They helped me break out of my shell.

One of the biggest highlights of my career came when LinkedIn invited us to share our success story. We had been using their platform extensively, both free and paid tools, and they wanted to feature us.

It was a dream come true. I had seen LinkedIn's video case studies at major industry events and always imagined being part of one.

Initially, they proposed a written case study, which itself was exciting. But then they decided to turn it into a video case study, a moment of validation and recognition I had long hoped for.

Sanjay and the entire leadership team were thrilled. It was a proud milestone, not just for me, but for our entire team and everything we had worked so hard to accomplish.

Navigating High Pressure, Leadership Growth, and Self-Realization

Work was progressing at an impressive pace, we were achieving higher productivity, reducing costs, and improving efficiency. But this progress came at a cost. The pressure to deliver results quickly led to frequent conflicts with stakeholders, many of whom had known me for years.

Process and policy changes were necessary, but not always well received. Sanjay, ever the strategist, handled these tensions and encouraged me to stay aggressive in my approach.

With his mentorship and my execution, we were driving real impact. Senior leadership was pleased with my work, and then came a defining moment. Our LinkedIn case study was published.

It was a huge achievement, making us the first mid-sized company to be featured, and it gave me unexpected visibility in the Talent Acquisition community.

Then, Sanjay announced his departure. His decision to leave was sudden and shocking for the entire team. His absence created a leadership vacuum, and my reporting structure changed.

I now reported directly to the India Managing Director, someone who knew and appreciated my work. While he provided valuable feedback on conflict management and stakeholder relationships, I quickly realized there was still so much to learn.

My expertise in sourcing was solid, and we continued to meet our hiring targets. However, I struggled with relationship management which is a crucial skill in recruitment. I was seen as aggressive, harsh, and too direct, and while I knew it was true, anxiety made it difficult to adjust my approach.

We introduced a scalable, paperless off-campus recruiting tool, which was well received, but internally, I continued to wrestle with my rigid work style. I built strong relationships with my clients and team, yet recruitment, at its core, is a service function that requires a balance of assertiveness and receptivity, something I still hadn't mastered. Asking for help might have been the key, but I wasn't ready to admit it.

My visibility in the company was strong. I had worked closely with key senior executives during my US stint and was seen as someone who could execute and deliver results. But after 10 years, I started wondering if it was time for a change.

That's when I got a call from a headhunter. The opportunity sounded exciting, sparking thoughts of exploring something new. But with that excitement came self-doubt and anxiety, could I leave behind everything I had built?

Determined to improve before making any decisions, I hired an external coach and immersed myself in leadership studies. Our company library was full of resources, and two Harvard Business Review articles resonated deeply with me:

"Save Your Rookie Manager from Himself"

"Manage Your Energy, Not Your Time"

Despite my increasing visibility and professional success, my inner restlessness never faded. I wasn't the only one feeling the pressure. Everyone was struggling in their own way. But instead of dealing with it, I buried myself in work, excessive reading, and constant travel, unintentionally neglecting my family.

Switching off felt impossible. My mind was wired for stress. Always searching for the next problem to solve. Even minor disagreements felt like personal attacks, triggering extreme reactions. My coach pointed this out and gave me a crucial insight:

"Dealing with imperfection isn't a weakness—it's your job as a leader."

That realization hit me hard. For the first time, I started to see that leadership wasn't just about expertise and execution. It was about adaptability, emotional intelligence, and balance.

And now, with a promising new opportunity on the horizon, I had to decide: stay where I was comfortable or take a leap into the unknown?

With my growing involvement in social volunteer work, I was entrusted with a senior position that required a greater time commitment. IT Milan, the IT wing of the IT Workers' Sangh, had expanded significantly, nearly achieving the ambitious goals we had set.

However, one persistent challenge remained—high volunteer attrition. Many people would join enthusiastically, contribute for a week or two, and then disappear without a word. Despite this, our contact list had grown exponentially.

People frequently reached out to me seeking assistance for various causes, particularly education for underprivileged students. Realizing the potential of our expanding network, I decided to experiment. Whenever an inquiry for help came in, I sent a message to our entire list.

The response was overwhelming. In no time, we had more commitments than we needed.

This was a breakthrough moment. Most of our members were well-paid IT professionals who genuinely wanted to contribute but found it difficult to commit time due to their demanding careers. Financial contributions, however, were much easier for them.

Recognizing this as a scalable model, I formalized it into a structured process—every time a new request came in, we tapped into our network, and the results were consistent. Thanks to my personal brand and strong rapport within IT Milan, we never faced a shortage of support.

Surprisingly, internal resistance emerged from within Milan itself. Some leaders were hesitant about this new approach, fearing a shift from traditional volunteer work. However, with the Noida Head's endorsement, we moved forward.

Over the next 10 years, this initiative helped a significant number of students, proving that leveraging collective goodwill in the right way could create real, lasting impact.

A Decade of Growth and a Bold Leap Forward

By 2014, I was nearing 10 years with my company, and things were going well. As part of my role, I traveled to our Ukraine office, meeting the team and gaining valuable insights. The trip was exciting, though the bitter cold of January made it quite an experience.

While I was in the Ukraine, I received a call from a headhunter about an exciting opportunity. It was a well-known startup on a strong growth trajectory. Intrigued, I decided to explore it further and was ultimately selected. The company was smaller in scale but had tremendous potential.

At the same time, I received other offers from competitor companies, each with lucrative packages and additional perks like stock options. However, doubt remained. I wasn't entirely sure if leaving was the right move.

I sought advice from my network, including colleagues and mentors, and received mixed opinions. Some encouraged me to take the leap, while others suggested I stay put. A Jumba alumnus pushed me to step out of my comfort zone. After much deliberation, I decided to take the plunge and resign.

Mood swings in anxiety can be dangerous, as they often cloud judgment and lead to impulsive decisions. In my case, the company tried to retain me, offering incentives to stay, but I was in a different state of mind, driven by a mix of overconfidence, restlessness, and a desire to escape certain professional challenges.

This emotional volatility made me overlook the long-term implications of my actions. Looking back, I realized that taking big risks feels different after a decade of stability, and it's crucial to validate these emotional shifts to make more grounded decisions.

Meanwhile, a significant event was unfolding in my family. My father won a landmark Supreme Court case, reinstating him with full seniority and benefits as the General Manager of his plant. His legal battle had lasted years, but truth prevailed. He was awarded all back wages and increments, making his case a historic judgment in India's co-operative employment sector.

With major transitions happening both personally and professionally, I stepped into my new role, ready to embrace the unknown, unaware of the challenges that lay ahead.

As I prepared to join my new company, I decided to take another meditation retreat. Someone suggested a new course, and despite its steep cost, I enrolled. It was a two-day program, and I found it refreshing.

Before my transition, my team and colleagues gave me a memorable farewell party, a moment of gratitude for all the years we had spent together. Rajiv, one of my closest colleagues, was also making the move with me, which felt reassuring.

However, reality hit soon after joining. The company's next funding round was delayed, and a new CEO had taken over, implementing drastic changes. At first, we assumed this was temporary turbulence, but soon, layoffs began. Hiring slowed to a trickle, and uncertainty loomed.

Initially, I kept my composure, but anxiety took over. Panic attacks and negative thinking became frequent. Being in a new environment after 10 years of stability was daunting. Adjusting to new colleagues, new ways of working, and a product-based company's culture was more difficult than I had anticipated.

With layoffs increasing and hiring grinding to a halt, I feared that I, too, might be on the chopping block. My anxiety skyrocketed. I started questioning everything—had my success been a fluke? Had I made a huge mistake leaving my old job? My confidence began to erode.

Desperate for a backup plan, I started job hunting again. I even considered starting a recruiting services business, but the risk was too high, so I set it aside.

I also had an idea for a predictive analytics-based recruiting tool—a system that would create a talent bell curve using a company's existing workforce and a code review algorithm to predict candidate fitment. Psychometric tests could further streamline hiring. However, I lacked the technical expertise to build it.

I reached out to multiple entrepreneurs and tech professionals working on similar ideas, but no one shared my exact vision. Eventually, I joined the advisory board of a startup, but unfortunately, it failed.

The sudden instability pushed me into deep fear and panic. Sleep became difficult, and I found myself stuck in a negative thought loop. In moments like these, thinking positively feels impossible, and breaking free seems out of reach.

To escape this cycle, I immersed myself in social work and meditation retreats. I attended a three-day workshop at the Paramhansa Yogananda Center in Noida, hoping for clarity.

After weighing my options, I accepted an offer from a Knowledge Process Outsourcing (KPO) firm, turning down opportunities at a leading startup and a product services company. Having witnessed the volatility of early-stage companies, I was now hesitant to take that risk.

Around the same time, I introduced Sanjay to one of the firms I had been in discussions with, and he later joined as their Global HR Head. Meanwhile, I was drawn to the high-finance outsourcing market that my new company specialized in.

I even reached out to my previous employer to explore a potential return, but at that time, no suitable roles were available.

As I settled into my new role, Pragati and Yashi expressed a desire to move back to the US, having lived there before and missing the experience. I, too, wanted to explore opportunities abroad, but making an international transition through a new employer was challenging. Despite the hurdles, I began exploring possibilities.

This job was a completely different ballgame—a larger scale, a new industry, and global exposure to markets like China, LATAM, and Eastern Europe.

The outgoing leader, who had referred me for this role, ensured a smooth transition. Interestingly, we had interacted for 5-7 years virtually but met in person for the first time. It was a testament to the power of professional networks.

However, with this new opportunity came a significant challenge—a long and exhausting commute. Despite hiring a driver, the one-way journey often stretched to two hours. But the company was in growth mode, and I had my work cut out for me. Social media strategy, sourcing automation, and process efficiency were my key focus areas.

The existing team was strong, but accepting a new leader wasn't easy for them. Some difficult personnel decisions had to be made, which caused some friction.

I jumped into execution mode, expanding the team and even bringing in Rajiv. Convincing my boss to hire him took effort, but he went on to build a long and successful career with the company.

The most exciting projects included Global Automation, social media adoption, and trainng development. One of my passion projects was the "Cognitive Barriers in Interviewing" training, which I had designed in a previous role. We enhanced it with Behavioral Event Interviewing (BEI) and rolled it out across our global offices.

We saw improvements in key metrics like turnaround time and cost efficiency, but I found myself missing the fast-paced IT skill-based hiring I had done before.

Despite the career growth, I continued to experience panic attacks and an overwhelming fear of the unknown.

To shift my perspective, I proposed and facilitated a two-day workshop on "Appreciative Inquiry"—a powerful, positive approach to problem-solving and leadership development. It was a transformational experience, giving me a fresh outlook on challenges.

Having Rajiv by my side was a comfort, and I had strong relationships within the company, but the internal struggle never stopped.

Key Insights

1. **Anxiety doesn't just stay in the background—it impacts performance & growth**

   ◦ The hesitation in meetings, fear of failure, and imposter syndrome should be more explicit.

2. **Marriage & work-life balance is not just about time—it's about emotional presence**

   ◦ The struggle of emotionally disengaging from work, carrying stress into the home, and learning to be present is a key theme.

3. **Work becomes a coping mechanism, but at a cost**

- The tendency to overwork as an escape from anxiety, personal struggles, or self-doubt should be deepened.

4. **Mentorship & guidance can shift perspective in powerful ways**

   - The impact of mentors like Sanjay on professional confidence and anxiety management should be more emotionally resonant.

Reflect and Act

1. Think about your professional journey – Identify three major work challenges you've faced and how you coped with them. This helps in recognizing strengths and areas for growth.

1. Identify a key lesson from early career experiences – Consider how past workplace challenges have shaped your ability to handle pressure and uncertainty today.
2. Identify hidden stressors – Determine the biggest sources of stress in your work life and whether you're managing them effectively.
3. Shift your perspective – Reflect on how you've adapted to major challenges at work and what strategies helped you navigate uncertainty.
4. Assess your work-life balance – Evaluate whether deadlines, meetings, or performance pressure are overwhelming and identify small adjustments for a healthier balance.

5. Consider your workplace culture – Assess whether your
    work environment supports mental well-being or
    normalizes burnout, and think about ways to contribute
    to a more supportive culture.

Work-life balance and emotional well-being don't
happen overnight, but small shifts in mindset and action
can lead to meaningful change.

****

CHAPTER 6. CONFRONTING ANXIETY IN THE PRESENT

""Our anxiety does not come from thinking about the future, but from wanting to control it."- Kahlil Gibran"

A Leap of Faith

In 2016, I began exploring international opportunities and reached out to my professional and alumni networks across the U.S., MENA, and the U.K. Soon, multiple offers came my way. However, I felt a strong pull to reconnect with my previous employer, where I had spent a decade growing both personally and professionally.

I reached out to the CEO, and to my surprise, the response was immediate. The timing was perfect. The company was looking for someone to lead their rapidly growing telecom business in the U.S., a domain I had successfully handled during my earlier tenure in both India and the U.S.

What made the offer even more appealing was the promise of a faster route to permanent residency, given the leadership role. It felt like everything was falling into place.

The opportunity aligned with my experience, the company knew me well and had accepted me with all my strengths and imperfections. It felt like coming home, and as a family, we were all excited for this new chapter. Everything seemed perfect.

Within a week I was offered and was asked to relocate to US within 6 weeks. But relocating within just a month and a half was a massive undertaking.

Getting a visa appointment was a challenge in itself. Time was slipping away. I had only 25 days left before I'd lose eligibility. We went into overdrive. It felt like everyone - HR, Immigration, and Operations was working around the clock to make it happen.

Pragati and Yashi were thrilled, and even little Mishi, after watching countless videos and photos of our soon-to-be new home, was looking forward to the move.

Finally, my visa was approved; though not without some tough questions at the interview. The three applicants before me had been rejected, but I was well-prepared and got through. Everything was happening exactly as I had envisioned.

I resigned from my job and prepared for the big move. Our destination: Dallas, Texas. The city housed some of our company's largest clients, and I was taking on a critical role, managing the telecom business, a domain I had successfully led before.

The work was intense, but I already knew many of the key players, having either hired them or worked with them in the past.

The Reality of a Fresh Start

Despite my excitement, doubts started creeping in. Hiring in the U.S. was an entirely different ballgame, and I had been out of touch with the market for six years. Unlike my leadership roles in the past, this job required me to be a hands-on individual contributor while building my offshore team.

I tried to suppress my anxiety and push forward, but it found ways to surface. Thankfully, an industry colleague, Prabir, was based in Dallas. We had met through IT Milan, and he, along with a Saint Paul's classmate, helped me settle in. Prabir even booked our apartment before we arrived. The IT Milan network was strong in the U.S. as well, and within two to three weeks, we were all set.

Work started immediately. I met key clients and was introduced to industry seniors who provided invaluable guidance. But the pressure was immense. While building my team in India, I had to personally close roles in the U.S. It had been a while since I worked hands-on, and my anxiety took a wild turn. I became obsessed with meeting targets. Even after office hours, my mind was consumed with worst-case scenarios leading to severe palpitations, chest tightness, and sweating.

Pragati noticed and, one day, told me bluntly: *"I feel defeated by your anxiety."* It was a statement that hit hard. Despite closing positions at record speed and keeping my boss happy, I felt constantly paranoid like everything could come crashing down at any moment.

This fear affected my interactions with colleagues. Sometimes I came across as aggressive, other times as uncertain and hesitant.

A Shift in Mindset

Something had to change. Drawing from my learnings in meditation and Appreciative Inquiry, I started focusing on what was within my control. I accepted situations as they were, rather than spiraling into "*what-ifs.*"

My priority became developing my team—mentoring them, helping them see the bigger picture, and earning their respect before leading them.

By the third month, I had built my full team. The night shift in India was grueling, but together, we made steady progress. True to their promise, the company filed my PR application on an expedited path. I kept up with my meditation, using it as a tool to manage my anxiety.

After a year, my boss Sonia left, and a new leader took over a seasoned professional with two decades of experience. Things were going well, but then, out of nowhere, disaster struck.

My PR application was denied due to a technicality.

The Devastation of a Broken Dream

We had met the rehire criteria, but a subclause required a re-entry into the U.S. A detail that had been overlooked by multiple attorneys. My long-term plan was suddenly shattered. Pragati and Yashi were in shock. Mishi was too young to understand, but I was drowning in anxiety.

In a desperate attempt to find a solution, I requested my boss and the Global Talent Head to transfer me to an H1B visa, which they did. We even explored options in other countries. Even then, my H1B visa had hurdles, but eventually, it was approved. We decided to stay.

Yet, with the PR path indefinitely stalled, I found it incredibly difficult to manage my anxiety. I felt directionless, stuck in negative self-talk that clouded my ability to think clearly. It affected my work, my motivation, and my ability to lead.

Over the years, my permanent residency application was filed three times, and my H1B visa faced two rejections before finally being approved. It felt like I kept hitting an invisible wall, perhaps a sign of divine will or destiny at play, though accepting it was never easy.

The Mental Battle

Despite finally securing my visa, the weight of uncertainty never lifted. Without a clear path to permanent residency, I struggled to stay motivated. Negative self-talk crept in, clouding my thinking, and I felt like I was slowly losing my footing.

Work, which had always been my refuge, began to feel heavy. The lack of clarity about my future made it difficult to stay fully engaged, and I worried it would start to affect not just me, but my team as well.

We tried filing for permanent residency three times — and each time, we hit a wall. My H1B visa itself was approved only after two failed attempts. I felt stuck, with no clear way forward.

At times, I wondered if this was life's way of pushing me toward something I hadn't yet considered. It was painful to

accept, but deep down, I knew that while I couldn't control
the circumstances, I could control my response.

So, I chose to shift my focus. Instead of spiraling into
frustration, I poured my energy into mentoring my team —
helping them grow into future leaders. If my own path felt
uncertain, I would create certainty for others.

Drawing on everything I had learned from
Organizational Behaviour, my time with IT Milans, and the
Appreciative Inquiry method, I set out to transform my
team.

The challenges were real. My entire team was offshore,
working the tough night shifts, with limited exposure
beyond sourcing. In the competitive world of U.S.
recruiting, they were under immense pressure.

The first step was clarity setting a vision for the team
and each individual. Having personally hired most of them,
I knew their strengths and weaknesses. I decided to be
honest and vulnerable with them about my own struggles
with chronic anxiety. I wanted them to know that even
leaders have doubts and bad days. I first shared this with
my senior team members Krish, Abhi, and Shashi.

Together, we set ambitious goals, using Appreciative
Inquiry to encourage everyone to become masters of their
craft. I even broke industry norms by assigning key
accounts to team members, empowering them to manage
independently. This was unheard of, but it worked. We
kicked off the transformation with an intense sourcing
workshop, where we built processes from the ground up.

Most learning happened live through real projects,
storytelling, and on-the-job mentoring. There were bumps
along the way, but we faced them together.

Leadership changes came and went. Each time, I had to
adjust, but by then, I had learned the art of adaptability.

When Shruti, my new boss, came on board, I chose to be open with her too. She became one of the most supportive leaders I've worked with helping me untangle many misconceptions I had built about myself and how leadership saw me.

The results over the years told a powerful story. In an industry known for high turnover, only five people left our team in nine years, a testament to the culture we had built together.

Even those who did move on found success, stepping into leadership roles at some of the top companies in the industry.

I had forged strong relationships with my immediate bosses, though navigating peer relationships continued to be an area of personal growth.

On a larger scale, the company itself soared to record-breaking market capitalization, something I felt proud to have contributed to.

In November 2024, I reached a personal milestone completing 20 years with the organization. It felt both surreal and humbling.

Outside of work, life moved along steadily. We settled into our new home, Yashi began her college journey, and Mishi celebrated her 13th birthday — small, joyful markers of time passing.

And quietly, my own journey with anxiety reached its 25th year — a reminder that while some battles remain with us, they can coexist with growth, achievement, and forward momentum.

Has the anxiety gone away?

No.

But I've learned to live with it, manage it, and even draw strength from it.

As William James said: *"The greatest weapon against stress is our ability to choose one thought over another."*

Key Insights

1. **Control is an illusion**

   - The realization that wanting to control the future is the root of anxiety is a profound theme. The struggle with visa applications, work pressures, and leadership changes highlights how uncertainty is a constant in life.
   - The key takeaway: *rather than trying to control everything, focus on responding constructively to change.*

2. **Leadership means empowering others**

   - True leadership isn't about personal success but about developing people.
   - By shifting focus from self-growth to team growth, the author regained purpose, showing how mentorship can be an antidote to anxiety.

3. **Vulnerability creates connection**

   - Opening up about anxiety with the team and new boss strengthened relationships. This shows that leaders don't have to be perfect to be respected.

4. **Adapting to setbacks is a superpower**

- Whether dealing with visa denials, corporate restructuring, or shifting career plans, the ability to pivot without losing momentum is a valuable skill.

Reflect and Act

1. **Identify Your Stressors at Work or Life**

   - What personal or workplace uncertainties trigger your anxiety? (e.g., leadership changes, job security, performance pressure)
   - How do you typically react to them? Are there alternative ways to cope?

2. **Shift Your Focus to Mentorship**

   - Can you shift your mindset from individual achievement to helping others grow?
   - Who in your workplace can benefit from your guidance, support, or encouragement?

3. **Assess Your Response to Setbacks**

   - Think about a time when something didn't go as planned. How did you react?
   - If you could reframe that experience, what would you do differently?

4. **Evaluate Your Work-Life Balance**

   - Is work taking up too much mental space?

- What small changes can you make to create better
boundaries between work and personal life?

****

Chapter 7. Beyond the Journey – Helping You Understand Anxiety

Anxiety is often a silent struggle, one that many battle alone, unsure of how to explain it to others. It can feel isolating, frustrating, and even overwhelming at times.

But the truth is, understanding anxiety is not just about personal healing; it's also about helping others navigate their own journey.

Through my experiences, I've learned that awareness and education can make a significant difference—not just for those who suffer from anxiety but also for the people around them.

Family, friends, colleagues, and even society at large often misunderstand anxiety, brushing it off as mere stress or overthinking. But real anxiety is deeper, more persistent, and can impact every aspect of life.

This chapter is about going beyond personal coping strategies. It's about breaking the stigma, creating awareness, and offering support—whether it's for a friend, a loved one, or even a colleague struggling in silence. By understanding anxiety better, we can become a source of strength for those who need it the most.

Effective Strategies to Cope with Chronic Anxiety

Managing chronic anxiety is an ongoing process that requires self-awareness, proactive effort, and the right mindset. Here are some powerful strategies that have helped me navigate through it:

1.Meditation

Practicing meditation regularly helps calm the mind, reduce stress, and improve focus. It creates a sense of inner peace and allows you to gain better control over anxious thoughts.

2.Asking for Help

Anxiety often makes us feel like we need to handle everything alone. Reaching out to trusted friends, coaches, mentors, psychologists or other medical experts can provide valuable support and perspective.

3.Surrounding Yourself with Positive People

Being in the company of optimistic and solution-oriented individuals helps shift your mindset. Observing how they handle challenges can inspire confidence and reduce negative thinking.

4.Identifying Anxiety Triggers

Understanding situations that make you nervous allows you to prepare better. Whether it's public speaking, high-pressure work scenarios, or social interactions, self-awareness is the first step toward managing reactions effectively.

5.Opening Up to Key People

Confiding in a few trusted colleagues or loved ones about your struggles creates a support system. Having people who understand your challenges can make a significant difference in dealing with anxiety.

6.Acting Brave Even When You Feel Anxious

Sometimes, the best way to overcome anxiety is to push through it. Hiding fear and taking action regardless helps build resilience over time. Eventually, what once seemed overwhelming becomes more manageable.

7.Developing Genuine Interest in Others

Focusing on building meaningful relationships and understanding others' perspectives shifts attention away from internal worries. Engaging deeply in conversations fosters stronger connections and reduces self-doubt.

8.Striving for Professional Excellence

Channelling energy into professional growth and mastering your craft builds confidence. Passion for excellence not only enhances career success but also provides a sense of control, counteracting feelings of helplessness that often accompany anxiety.

Each of these strategies has played a crucial role in managing my anxiety, helping me stay grounded and focused despite uncertainties. The key is consistency and self-compassion—progress happens step by step.

Things to Avoid When Coping with Anxiety

While there are many positive strategies to manage anxiety, certain habits can actually make it worse. Here are some things I've learned **not** to do—mistakes that can fuel overthinking, self-doubt, and unnecessary stress.

1.Over-Reading: Too Much Information, Too Little Action

It's tempting to read endlessly about anxiety, self-improvement, and mental health, hoping to find that one perfect solution. But too much reading without applying what you learn can lead to analysis paralysis.

Sometimes, taking action rather than consuming more information is what truly helps.

2.Avoid Speculative Activities: Don't Feed the Anxiety Beast

If you're already prone to overthinking, engaging in speculative activities, whether it's stock trading, predicting future events, or over-analyzing people's reactions can amplify your worries.

Uncertainty fuels anxiety, and constantly seeking certainty in unpredictable situations only worsens it.

3.Reading Too Much Philosophy or Psychology: A Double-Edged Sword

Deep intellectual topics like philosophy and psychology can be fascinating, but overindulging in them, especially during anxious phases can push you further into self-doubt.

Instead of finding clarity, you may end up questioning everything, leading to more confusion and stress. Keep it balanced.

4.Don't Chase Perfection: It's a Trap

Anxiety often convinces us that we must get everything just right—whether it's work, relationships, or even our personal growth journey. But perfection is an illusion. Instead of aiming for flawless, aim for progress. Accepting "good enough" can be liberating.

5.Stop Comparing Yourself with Others

Nothing fuels self-doubt like scrolling through social media or hearing about someone else's success and thinking: *Why am I not there yet?* Everyone has their own journey. Instead of comparing, focus on your own growth and wins, no matter how small.

6.Avoid Self-Diagnosing Anxiety and Depression

Reading too much about mental health disorders without professional guidance can lead to misconceptions and unnecessary panic. It's easy to start believing *I have all these symptoms!* When, in reality, anxiety is just one part of a bigger picture. Always seek expert advice rather than self-diagnosing.

7.Be Selective About Who You Share Your Struggles With

While opening up is important, discussing your anxiety with the wrong people—those who don't understand or who invalidate your feelings—can make things worse.

Choose a trusted circle of friends, mentors, or professionals who genuinely support you. Sometimes re-connecting with spirituality might help.

Managing anxiety is as much about what you avoid as it is about what you *actively do.* Cutting out these negative habits can create more mental space for peace, productivity, and self-growth.

The key is balance—stay informed, but don't overconsume; work hard, but don't chase perfection; share your struggles, but with the right people.

When Stress Crosses the Line: Know When to Seek Help and How to Keep It in Check

Stress is a normal part of life.

In fact, a little bit of stress is actually good—it pushes us to meet deadlines, stay motivated, and improve ourselves.

But what happens when stress goes beyond a healthy level?

How do you know when it's turning into chronic anxiety or something more serious?

The key lies in handling stress without letting it consume you.

Check in with yourself, recognize the signs, and make changes before it spirals out of control with the following tips:

1.Normal Stress vs. Overwhelming Stress

We all experience stress—before an important meeting, a big exam, or even when making decisions.

But when stress starts interfering with your daily life, relationships, or health, it's a red flag.

Signs Your Stress is Becoming Too Much:

- You feel anxious or restless all the time
- You have trouble sleeping or frequently feel exhausted
- You overthink every situation, even small ones
- You experience mood swings, irritability, or frequent negative thoughts
- You feel overwhelmed even by simple tasks
- You withdraw from friends, family, or activities you once enjoyed

If you're experiencing several of these symptoms, it's time to take a step back and seek help whether from a trusted friend, a mentor, or a professional.

2.Don't Overcomplicate Life: Avoid the Philosophy Trap

While deep thinking and intellectual discussions can be enriching, too much focus on philosophy, psychology, or complex issues can actually increase anxiety—especially if you're already feeling overwhelmed.

It's okay to be curious, but don't lose yourself in over analysing life. Not every problem needs a deep existential answer. Sometimes, the best thing to do is take a break, go for a walk, or simply enjoy the moment.

3.Take It Easy: Life is Not a Race

We often put too much pressure on ourselves—to be the best at work, to earn more, to be perfect in our personal lives. But setting unrealistic expectations leads to frustration and burnout.

- Learn to slow down
- Enjoy small wins
- Accept that mistakes happen
- Take breaks without guilt

Stress management is not about doing less, but about doing things with the right mindset.

4.Be Part of a Social Group: Stay Connected

Humans are social beings. When we isolate ourselves, stress and anxiety multiply. Being around people—friends, family, or even colleagues—helps us stay grounded.

- Join a community group, volunteer, or just spend time with positive people
- Talk to friends regularly—even a short chat can lift your mood

- Share your feelings—it's okay to ask for help

The right company can make a world of difference.

5.Prioritize Family Time: Kids and Loved Ones Matter More Than Work

It's easy to get caught up in work, responsibilities, and daily stressors. But spending time with your family—especially children—brings a unique kind of joy and emotional stability.

Why Family Time Helps Reduce Stress:

- Kids live in the moment—they remind you to laugh and enjoy simple things
- Family bonds create emotional security
- Sharing thoughts and feelings with loved ones reduces anxiety

A simple game with your kids, a conversation with your spouse, or a family dinner can be more therapeutic than hours of self-help reading.

6.Set Realistic Expectations: Stop Trying to Control Everything

A lot of stress comes from expecting too much—from yourself, from others, and from life in general.

- Accept that you cannot control everything
- Lower expectations from people. Everyone has their own struggles
- Focus on what you can change, and let go of the rest

The sooner you release unrealistic expectations, the more at peace you'll feel.

7.Forgive and Forget: Don't Carry Emotional Baggage

Holding onto grudges or reliving past mistakes only adds unnecessary stress. Learn to forgive—both yourself and others.

- Let go of old conflicts
- Understand that nobody is perfect
- Free yourself from unnecessary emotional burdens

Forgiveness is not about excusing bad behaviour. It's about choosing your own peace of mind.

8.Ethics and Kindness: The Simple Secret to a Stress-Free Life

A lot of internal stress comes from guilt, dishonesty, or unresolved conflicts. The simplest way to live without anxiety? Be ethical. Be kind. Treat people well.

- Do the right thing, even when no one is watching
- Avoid office politics and unnecessary conflicts
- Be respectful, even when you disagree

The more integrity you have in your actions, the less you'll have to worry about hidden stressors.

9.Find Purpose in Helping Others

One of the best ways to manage stress is to shift the focus from yourself to helping others.

- Mentor someone at work
- Teach a skill to someone in need
- Help colleagues grow professionally

Seeing others succeed because of your guidance creates a deep sense of fulfillment and reduces self-doubt.

10.Don't Be Afraid to Ask for Help

Stress becomes dangerous when we try to handle everything alone. There's no shame in seeking support.

- Talk to someone—a friend, mentor, or therapist
- Accept that everyone needs help sometimes
- Build a support system—you don't have to figure everything out alone

Sometimes, a simple conversation can ease weeks of built-up stress.

11.Parents, Look Out for Early Signs of Stress in Kids

Children today face immense pressure—academically, socially, and emotionally. Parents play a crucial role in recognizing early signs of stress and providing support.

- Be aware of sudden mood changes
- Encourage open conversations about their feelings
- Provide reassurance without pressuring them

A child who feels heard and supported is less likely to carry stress into adulthood.

12. Stop Comparing Yourself to Others

Social media makes it easy to feel like you're falling behind. But everyone has their own struggles. People just don't post them online.

- Focus on your journey, not someone else's timeline
- Avoid unnecessary competition—life is not a contest
- Appreciate what you have, instead of what you lack

The moment you stop comparing, you free yourself from unnecessary pressure.

Stress is normal. But when it starts controlling your life, it's time to take a step back and reassess. By keeping things simple, staying connected with loved ones, setting realistic expectations, and focusing on what truly matters, you can keep stress in check and live a more balanced, fulfilling life. And most importantly, never hesitate to ask for help.

Key Insights

1. **Anxiety is a shared experience, not just an individual struggle**

   - The chapter emphasizes that anxiety is often misunderstood, not just by those who suffer from it but also by family, friends, and colleagues.
   - Breaking the stigma and raising awareness helps create a more supportive environment for those struggling.

2. **The importance of proactive strategies**

   - The section on effective coping mechanisms highlights meditation, seeking help, and surrounding oneself with positive influences.
   - These strategies reinforce that managing anxiety is a continuous process, not a one-time fix.

3. **What not to do matters as much as what to do**

   - Many people unknowingly worsen their anxiety by engaging in unhelpful behaviours like over-reading self-help books, chasing perfection, or over-analyzing situations.

- The chapter's breakdown of these negative habits provides practical insights into avoiding anxiety traps.

4. **Recognizing when stress becomes chronic anxiety**

- The discussion on normal vs. Overwhelming stress is particularly helpful for working professionals, offering clear red flags to identify when anxiety is taking over.
- This helps differentiate between healthy pressure that drives performance and toxic stress that leads to burnout.

5. **The role of work-life balance in mental health**

- The chapter highlights how family time, social connections, and personal well-being should not be sacrificed for work.
- Learning to prioritize, set boundaries, and avoid over-commitment is key to long-term emotional resilience.

6. **Helping others as a path to self-healing**

- One of the most unique insights is that mentoring, guiding others, and engaging in social work can help ease personal anxiety.
- Shifting focus outward reduces self-doubt and negative thinking, reinforcing a sense of purpose.

Reflect and Act

1. **Support Someone Who Might Be Struggling**

   - Think of a colleague, friend, or family member who might be experiencing anxiety. How can you create a safe space for them to talk about their struggles?
   - Could you offer mentorship, emotional support, or simply a listening ear?

2. **Identify Your Own Anxiety Triggers at Work**

   - What situations, people, or deadlines make you feel most anxious?
   - How do you currently react, and what changes can you make to handle them better?

3. **Assess Your Work-Life Balance**

   - Are you overcommitted at work?
   - Do you regularly set aside time for relaxation, hobbies, and family? If not, what one small change can you make this week to improve your balance?

4. **Reduce Unhelpful Habits**

   - Are you caught in any of the anxiety traps mentioned (e.g., over-reading, perfectionism, overanalysing situations)?
   - How can you shift from excessive thinking to taking meaningful action?

5. Embrace Imperfection & Let Go of Control

- What is one aspect of your life where you can practice letting go of unrealistic expectations?
- How can you reframe challenges as learning opportunities instead of failures?

****

CHAPTER NINE

CONCLUSION

As I reflect on this journey — both in life and in writing this book — one truth stands out: anxiety is not something we overcome once and for all. It is something we learn to live with, understand, and manage. For over 25 years, anxiety has been a silent companion in my life — sometimes loud and overwhelming, sometimes quietly lingering in the background. But through it all, I've discovered that anxiety does not have to define us or dictate the course of our lives.

This book was never meant to be just about my story. It is about every working professional who has felt the weight of unspoken fears, every family member who watches someone they love struggle in silence, and every leader who juggles expectations while battling self-doubt. It is about recognizing that behind professional success or confident appearances, there can still be vulnerability — and that's okay.

If there is one key message I hope stays with you, it is this: you are not alone. Whether you are navigating anxiety yourself or supporting someone who is, understanding and compassion can create lasting change. The tools and reflections shared in this book are not magic solutions, but they are small steps that can help you gain clarity, build resilience, find peace, and most importantly — achieve balance between work and life.

Remember:

- You don't need to have all the answers.
- Asking for help is a sign of strength, not weakness.
- Taking care of your mental and emotional well-being is just as important as meeting deadlines or achieving professional goals.

I encourage you to pause often, reflect on your experiences, and use the exercises provided in each chapter. Make time for meditation, stay connected with your support system, and most of all — be kind to yourself.

Life will always be uncertain. Challenges will come and go. But with the right mindset, tools, and support, you can choose how to respond.

Thank you for allowing me to share my journey with you. If this book has given you even a little hope, a moment of clarity, or the courage to start a conversation — then it has served its purpose.

Stay mindful. Stay resilient. Stay hopeful.

Wishing you strength, balance, and peace, always.

— Yuvraj Bhatnagar

CHAPTER TEN

ABOUT THE AUTHOR

Yuvraj Bhatnagar is a corporate professional, writer, and mental health advocate with over 25 years of experience navigating chronic anxiety. Having built a successful career in Talent Acquisition, he understands firsthand the pressures of high-performance environments and the toll they take on mental well-being.

A deep thinker with an analytical mind, Yuvraj has spent years studying psychology, meditation, and holistic healing techniques to manage anxiety. His journey from a childhood shaped by academic pressures and social anxiety to overcoming a severe nervous breakdown during his MBA has given him profound insights into the realities of living with chronic anxiety while striving for personal and professional success.

Through this book "The Silent Battle: My Story of Dealing with Chronic Anxiety," Yuvraj shares his lived experiences, offering readers an honest, relatable, and practical perspective on anxiety, resilience, and self-discovery. His work is a testament to the fact that while anxiety may never fully disappear, it can be understood, managed, and even transformed into a source of strength.

Beyond writing, Yuvraj is passionate about mentorship, personal development, and creating awareness about mental health in professional spaces. He believes in breaking the stigma around anxiety and hopes to empower others by fostering open conversations about mental well-being.

The author now dedicates his free time on weekends to helping working executives struggling with anxiety regain control over their lives. Through personalized consultations, he guides professionals in managing stress, building resilience, and achieving a healthier work-life balance. Drawing from his own experiences, he provides practical strategies to navigate workplace pressures while maintaining mental well-being.

He enjoys reading, exploring psychological concepts, and engaging in meaningful discussions about life, work, and human behaviour.

****

CHAPTER ELEVEN

Consultation for Working Executives Facing Chronic Anxiety

Struggling with workplace anxiety? You're not alone.

High-pressure environments, relentless deadlines, and career uncertainties can make anxiety feel overwhelming. If you're a working executive dealing with chronic anxiety and finding it difficult to balance work, personal life, and mental well-being, I invite you to a free 30-minute consultation where we can:

✓ Identify key anxiety triggers affecting your professional and personal life.

✓ Explore practical strategies to manage stress, overthinking, and burnout.

✓ Discuss ways to build resilience while maintaining peak

performance.

✔ Create a simple action plan to help you regain control and find clarity and balance.

This consultation is not therapy but a conversation based on real-life experience, practical solutions, and insights gained from years of managing anxiety in demanding corporate settings and find a work – life balance.

Book Your Free Consultation!

?? **Schedule a call**: yuvraj.bhatnagar@gmail.com

Your career should not come at the cost of your mental well-being. Let's work together to find a balance.

****

Appendices

Appendix A: Recommended Readings

- **"The Anxiety and Phobia Workbook" by Edmund J. Bourne:** A comprehensive guide offering practical tools and strategies to manage anxiety and phobias effectively.
- **"Dare: The New Way to End Anxiety and Stop Panic Attacks" by Barry McDonagh:** A revolutionary approach to overcoming anxiety and panic attacks by embracing and moving through fear.
- **"The Mindful Way Through Anxiety" by Susan M. Orsillo and Lizabeth Roemer:** A mindfulness-based guide to help individuals confront and manage anxiety with clarity and calm.
- **"When Panic Attacks" by David D. Burns:** A cognitive therapy-based book offering powerful techniques to defeat anxiety and panic without medication.
- **"Radical Acceptance" by Tara Brach:** A compassionate guide to embracing life fully, even in the face of suffering, through mindfulness and self-compassion.
- **"You Can Heal Your Life" by Louise Hay:** This book focuses on the power of affirmations and positive thinking to overcome physical and emotional challenges.
- **Eckhart Tolle**'s books, such as **"The Power of Now"** and **"A New Earth**," offer insights on living in the present moment and reducing anxiety.

Appendix B: Mental Health Organizations

- **National Alliance on Mental Illness (NAMI)**

  - Website:nami.org
  - Offers resources, support groups, and educational materials.

- **Anxiety and Depression Association of America (ADAA)**

  - Website:adaa.org
  - Provides information on anxiety, depression, and related disorders, including resources for treatment and support.

- **Mental Health America (MHA)**

  - Website:mhanational.org
  - Offers screening tools, support resources, and advocacy for mental health.

- **Mind (UK)**

  - Website:mind.org.uk
  - Provides advice and support to anyone experiencing a mental health problem.

Appendix C: Contact Information for Professional Help

- **National Suicide Prevention Lifeline (USA)**

  - Phone: 1-800-273-TALK (1-800-273-8255)
  - Website:suicidepreventionlifeline.org

- **Crisis Text Line**

  - Text HOME to 741741 (USA)
  - Website:crisistextline.org

- **Samaritans (UK)**

  - Phone: 116 123
  - Website:samaritans.org

- **Lifeline (Australia)**

  - Phone: 13 11 14
  - Website:lifeline.org.au

- **Vandrevala Foundation (India)**

  - Phone: 1860 266 2345 / 9999 666 555
  - Website: vandrevalafoundation.com

- **iCall - Tata Institute of Social Sciences (India)**

  - Phone: +91 9152987821
  - Email: icall@tiss.edu

- ○ Website: icallhelpline.org

- **Kids Help (Canada)**

  - ○ Phone: 1-800-668-6868
  - ○ Website: kidshelpphone.ca

- **Canadian Mental Health Association (CMHA)**

  - ○ Website: cmha.ca
  - ○ Provides resources and support for mental health across Canada.

- **International Resources**

  - ○ Visit the International Association for Suicide Prevention (IASP) for a directory of helplines around the world: iasp.info/resources/ Crisis_Centres/

  o Befrienders Worldwide: Offers a global directory of emotional support helplines, including various countries in Asia. Website: befrienders.org

Appendix D: Other Resources

- **Marisa Peer Resources**

  - ○ Marisa Peer, a renowned therapist, offers programs and books on Rapid Transformational Therapy (RTT) to address anxiety and improve mental health.
  - ○ Website:marisapeer.com

- **The Art of Living Foundation**

  - Offers meditation, breathing exercises, and stress management programs to promote mental well-being.
  - Website:artofliving.org

- **Alpha Mind Power**

  o Srimatha Vijayalakshmi Panthaiyan offers workshops and classes and provides guidance on stress management, goal achievement, and positive thinking
  o Website: https://alphamindpower.net/
  o amp@alphamindpower.net or call +91 63796 91989.

- **Deepak Chopra Foundation**

  - Deepak Chopra's books and guided meditations focus on holistic health, mindfulness, and the mind-body connection.
  - Website:deepakchopra.com

- **Thich Nhat Hanh's Teachings**

  - Renowned Zen master Thich Nhat Hanh offers practical mindfulness exercises and teachings on peace and compassion.
  - Books: "The Miracle of Mindfulness," "Peace Is Every Step"

- **Headspace App**

  - A popular app offering guided meditations and

mindfulness exercises designed to reduce stress and anxiety.
- Website:headspace.com

- **Calm App**

  - Provides guided meditations, sleep stories, and relaxation techniques to help manage anxiety and improve sleep.
  - Website:calm.com

- **Tony Robbins** offers personalized coaching that includes strategies for overcoming anxiety, building confidence, and improving overall mental health.

****

References

1. https://www.who.int/news-room/fact-sheets/detail/anxiety-disorders

2. Evans-Lacko S, Aguilar-Gaxiola S, Al-Hamzawi A, et al. Socio-economic variations in the mental health treatment gap for people with anxiety, mood, and substance use disorders: results from the WHO World Mental Health (WMH) surveys. Psychol Med. 2018;48(9):1560-1571.

3. Charlson, F., van Ommeren, M., Flaxman, A., Cornett, J., Whiteford, H., & Saxena, S. New WHO prevalence estimates of mental disorders in conflict settings: a systematic review and meta-analysis. Lancet. 2019;394,240–248.

4. Javaid, S.F., Hashim, I.J., Hashim, M.J. et al. Epidemiology of anxiety disorders: global burden and sociodemographic associations. Middle East Curr Psychiatry 30, 44 (2023). https://doi.org/10.1186/s43045-023-00315-3

5. Spitzer RL, Kroenke K, Williams JBW, Löwe B. A brief measure for assessing generalized anxiety disorder: The GAD-7. Arch Intern Med. 2006;166:1092-7.

6. https://nmji.in/anxiety-disorders/#ref11

7. https://adaa.org/understanding-anxiety/facts-statistics

8. https://www.psychiatry.org/news-room/news-releases/annual-poll-adults-express-increasing-anxiousness

9. https://anxietychecklist.com/anxiety-statistics

10. Spill Chat – Workplace Mental Health Statistics

11. Lebowitz ER. Treating Anxiety in Kids by Working

With Parents. Child Mind Institute. Published August 2021. Accessed February 27, 2025.https://childmind.org/article/treating-anxiety-in-kids-by-working-with-parents/

12. Gibson L. Do you have an 'emotionally immature parent'? How a nine-year-old self-help book became a TikTok sensation. The Guardian. Published April 18, 2024. Accessed February 27, 2025.https://www.theguardian.com/wellness/2024/apr/18/emotionally-immature-parents

13. Sharma S, Sharma M. Parenting Styles as Correlates of Academic Anxiety among Adolescents. International Journal of Indian Psychology. 2015;2(2):102-109. Accessed February 27, 2025. https://ijip.in/articles/parenting-styles-as-correlates-of-academic-anxiety-among-adolescents/

14. Kessler RC, McLaughlin KA, Green JG, et al. Childhood adversities and adult psychopathology in the WHO World Mental Health Surveys. Br J Psychiatry. 2010;197(5):378-385. doi:10.1192/bjp.bp.110.080499. Accessed February 27, 2025. https://www.cambridge.org/core/journals/the-british-journal-of-psychiatry/article/childhood-adversities-and-adult-psychopathology-in-the-who-world-mental-health-surveys/

****